CHECK FOR
MAP IN
BACK POCKET

GL_____R ™

T_____ _de

KT-471-867

MALDIVES

STEFANIA LAMBERTI

NEW
HOLLAND

★★★ Highly recommended
★★ Recommended
★ See if you can

Fourth edition first published in 2004
by New Holland Publishers (UK) Ltd
London • Cape Town • Sydney • Auckland
First published in 1997
10 9 8 7 6 5 4 3 2 1

website: www.newhollandpublishers.com

Garfield House,
86 Edgware Road
London, W2 2EA
United Kingdom

80 McKenzie Street
Cape Town, 8001
South Africa

14 Aquatic Drive
Frenchs Forest, NSW 2086
Australia

218 Lake Road
Northcote, Auckland
New Zealand

Distributed in the USA by
The Globe Pequot Press,
Connecticut

Copyright © 2004 in text: Stefania Lamberti
Copyright © 2004 in maps: Globetrotter Travel Maps
Globetrotter Travel Maps
Copyright © 2004 in photographs:
Individual photographers as credited (right)
Copyright © 2004 New Holland Publishers (UK) Ltd

ISBN 1 84330 841 X

Although every effort has been made to ensure that
this guide is up to date and current at time of going
to print, the Publisher accepts no responsibility or
liability for any loss, injury or inconvenience incurred
by readers or travellers using this guide.

Publishing Manager (UK): Simon Pooley
Publishing Manager (SA): Thea Grobbelaar
DTP Cartographic Manager: Genené Hart
Editors: Melany McCallum, Mary Duncan, Nune
Jordaan, Susannah Coucher
Cartographers: Nicole Engeler, Genené Hart, John Hall,
William Smuts
Design and DTP: Gillian Black, Sonya Cupido
Consultants: Charles and Susan Anderson, Katerina
and Eric Roberts
Reproduction by Hirt & Carter (Pty) Ltd, Cape Town
Printed and bound by Times Offset (M) Sdn. Bhd.,
Malaysia.

Acknowledgements:
The list of people that helped me during my stays on
the islands is infinite. I thank them all. I must make
special mention of Mohamed Arif (Marketing Director
of Sun Travel and Tours) and Fatima Sigera (Marketing
Manager of Aqua Sun), their help was invaluable.
Also Ahmed Adil at the Ministry of Tourism.
Closer to home, I would like to thank my husband
Peter for his patience and Anne Layne for her help.

Keep us Current
Information in travel guides is apt to change, which is
why we regularly update our guides. We'd be grateful
to receive feedback if you've noted something we
should include in our updates. If you have new
information, please share it with us by writing to the
Publishing Manager, Globetrotter, at the office nearest
to you (addresses on this page). The most significant
contribution to each new edition will receive a free
copy of the updated guide.

Cover: *Thulhaagiri Island Resort.*
Title Page: *Maldives, a picture-book paradise.*

CONTENTS

1
Introducing Maldives

Imagine a whole country formed by aquatic animals. Such is the geological make-up of the Republic of Maldives. These small, idyllic islands, sprinkled on the surface of the deep Indian Ocean, owe their existence to the fervent work of minute coral polyps.

To the holiday-maker the islands evoke dreams of leaning **palm trees** and sparkling **turquoise seas** – a picture book paradise. Bungalows nestle discreetly in lush vegetation that lines the pearly **white beaches**. Beyond, the shallow lagoon offers the luxury of wallowing in the biggest swimming pool on earth. Swings hanging from palm trees offer a comfortable resting place in the cool shade. Peppering the **Indian Ocean** within the surfacing atoll reefs, **resort islands** alternate with local **fishing villages** where the people lead a simple yet comfortable existence. Friendly, but somewhat reserved in their ways, Maldivians are proud of their culture.

The islands' main attraction lies beneath the surface of the warm waters that gently lap the perfect beaches. The coral reefs of Maldives are considered by many experts as some of the best in the world and are certainly comparable to the beauty and colour of the Red Sea, and to the variety of marine life of the Great Barrier Reef.

The archipelago forms a natural barrier across the Indian Ocean between the latitudes of 7°6'30"N and 0°41'48"S and the longitudes of 72°32'30"E and 73°45' 54"E. Its nearest neighbours are India and Sri Lanka which lie northeast of the **Maldivian Archipelago**.

TOP ATTRACTIONS

*** **Sun, sea** and **sand:** year-round temperatures between 30°C (86°F) and 26°C (79°F).
*** **Idyllic islands:** escape to a dreamy paradise.
*** **Underwater:** coral gardens, awesome drop-offs, a rich diversity of marine life.
*** **Watersports:** excellent diving, snorkelling, sailing, windsurfing and parasailing.
*** **Excursions:** snorkelling and diving safaris, night and game fishing, island-hopping and Malé shopping trips.

Opposite: *The coral reefs provide many hours of diving pleasure for tourists.*

THE LAND

Most visitors to Maldives arrive by plane. As the aircraft slowly descends, you will find yourself staring at what seem to be floating smudges of oil paint dropped into the **Indian Ocean**. These are the beautiful atolls of the Maldives.

Within the **26 atolls** are approximately **1200 coral islands** (and hundreds of small sandbanks), the exact number depending greatly on the tides and the storms that can easily sweep existing islands away and create new ones. **Sandbanks** and **coral patches** that may be exposed during low tide, may be submerged six hours later at high tide. The total land area is about 298km² (115 sq miles), making it the smallest country in Asia. The islands lie along a chain of atolls that stretches 823km (510 miles) north to south, 130km (81 miles) wide and covering over 90,000km² (34,750 sq miles).

The Formation of the Maldivian Archipelago

There are several theories as to how the archipelago was formed. The most accepted theory is that of Charles Darwin, the world-renowned British naturalist.

About 100 million years ago, as India drifted away from Africa, a geothermal 'hot spot' was formed in mid-ocean. Volcanic eruptions occurred between two diverging plates of the earth's crust, eventually forming a ridge of volcanic mountains that cleared the surface of the ocean. Once the islands had stabilized, in warm, silt-free waters that teemed with nutrients favouring coral growth, coral polyps colonized the walls of the volcanoes.

As the landmasses subsided and submerged, coral reefs continued to grow upwards, forming rings around the original coastline, and atolls were formed. The reefs in line with the surface of the water became exposed at low tide. Debris and coral fragments were washed onto the exposed reefs by currents, waves and tides. Coconuts and seeds washed ashore and colonized the exposed coralline shores. Animals and birds found sanctuary on the newly-formed islands and the basis for a new land was created.

In 1934 an Anglo-Egyptian oceanographic expedition visited Maldives and the experiments that were carried out supported Darwin's theory. His theory was further substantiated in 1980 when a seismic survey was conducted near the island of **Bandos**, in **North Malé Atoll**. Tests concluded that a subsided volcanic base of the **Eocene Epoch** (38 to 53 million years ago) at 2100m (6890ft) supports the built-up layers of limestone that originated in the shallow waters. Today the islands make up less than 1% of Maldivian territory.

RESORT ISLANDS

The islands of Maldives are all very similar, but the ever-increasing number of resorts vary greatly in standard – from those that offer luxurious comfort to the more basic yet comfortable variety. Each island is a self-contained community with a modern infrastructure that includes a generator, water supply and desalinization plant, communications and accommodation. Most islands also have an incinerator to burn non-biodegradable rubbish. The size of the island can be determined by the minutes it takes to walk around it, on average under an hour!

Opposite: *Aerial view of the islands and lagoons that form an atoll.*
Left: *The water is so clear that one can easily distinguish the sand patches from the coral reefs.*

The Atolls

Maldivians were the first to use the word 'atoll'. In the
Dhivehi language, *atholhu* means a ring-shaped coral
island or reef surrounding a lagoon. Today the English
word is commonly used to describe this geographic
phenomenon worldwide. Like a floating garland, the
atolls form a double chain in the middle with a single
row of atolls to the north and south. Deep channels,
often swept by strong currents, separate the atolls.

The Maldives' 26 atolls rise from a common plateau
on the ocean floor that's as deep as 2500m (8203ft) on the
eastern side and 4000m (13,124ft) on the western side. In
comparison, the lagoon enclosed by atolls is flat and
sandy and relatively shallow, the deepest one not
reaching 100m (328ft). The sand in a lagoon originates
from the outer reefs. It is then carried into the atoll by
currents and tides sweeping through natural channels
that break an enclosure reef. Each atoll is a complex
system of reefs, channels, faros and islands. **Faros** are
those numerous smaller atolls rising from an atoll's floor
and making up each large one. Those that occur within
the lagoon of a large atoll are round, while those that
occur at the rim are elongated.

The Islands

The islands of Maldives are coralline, and so are typically flat, with the maximum height of the entire country no more than 3m (10ft) above sea level. Most islands occur close to an atoll enclosure reef and vary in size from a patch of sand to a fully developed island.

Covering their coral base, the older islands have accumulated a layer of soil made of decomposed vegetable and animal matter. These islands are now covered in lush, tropical vegetation with a naturally high water table; some islands even have fresh water.

Islands are protected from the harsh elements by a surrounding reef that normally encloses a shallow lagoon, while the ocean forces are kept at bay by an atoll's enclosure reef.

Village Islands

Apart from **Malé**, the capital city, the villages of the archipelago have not been influenced much by the Western world and they keep strictly to their Muslim faith. Each village island forms a close-knit and self-sufficient community. Traditionally a community may move to another, more populous island when there are less than 40 men attending Friday prayers, if disease and death spread through a village, or the island is eroded.

Above: *Streets, covered in coralline sand, are swept clean and the sand replaced by the local women.*

Opposite: *There are about 1200 coral islands in this mid-ocean chain, and only 200 are inhabited.*

Opposite: *The Maldives is an isolated group of islands and as such they have developed their own species of plant life.*

Most villages have at least two mosques, one for women and one for men, and a generator as well as rainwater storage tanks which are provided by the government.

On islands visited by tourists, local shops alternate with curio shops where lacquer work, jewellery, trinket boxes and *feli* cloths (cotton sarongs), reed mats (*kuuna*), hand-printed T-shirts, and imported woodwork are sold at reasonable prices. Teashops offer the typical Maldivian tea and, more recently, softdrinks.

Climate

Many people ask: 'When is it **monsoon** season?' What they probably mean to ask about is the **rainy season**. A monsoon is a wind, and each year Maldives is affected by **two monsoons**: *iruvai* (the northeast monsoon) is hot and dry, while *hulhangu* (the southwest monsoon) brings wind and rain.

The Maldives is an ideal holiday destination through-out the year, but the best time to visit is during the dry monsoon, between **November** and **April**, when blue skies and sunshine are most likely. During the low season, from **May** to **October**, the hot days are frequently broken by storms and tropical showers. Only the far northern atolls are struck by cyclones. Annual rainfall is approximately 1870mm (74 in).

Generally hot and humid, the days are made tolerable by a gentle, steady sea breeze. The temperature rarely drops below 25 °C (77 °F) and generally reaches the 30 °C (86 °F) mark. The water temperature fluctuates between 25 °C (77 °F) and 29 °C (84 °F), making Maldivian waters perfect for prolific coral growth.

MALDIVES	J	F	M	A	M	J	J	A	S	O	N	D
AVERAGE TEMP. °F	86	86	86	88	88	88	86	86	86	86	86	86
AVERAGE TEMP. °C	30	30	30	31	31	31	30	30	30	30	30	30
HOURS OF SUN DAILY	7.5	8.5	8.5	8	7.5	6.5	7.5	6.5	6.5	8	7.5	7
RAINFALL in	4.5	0.5	3.5	5	7	7	5	7.5	7	6	8	8
RAINFALL mm	121	46	96	123	178	177	131	192	182	161	209	206
DAYS OF RAINFALL	10	5	8	10	16	16	11	17	17	16	18	18

Plant Life

Due to their **coralline** nature, the Maldivian islands are not conducive to a diverse plant life. Although the older islands have developed an impervious layer of fine sand and clay which helps store rainwater, the soil is low in nutrients. As a result, trees like the coconut do well because they have a horizontal root system.

Plants of the islands are mainly **coconut trees**, **banyan**, **screwpine**, **vines** and **mangroves**. Closer to the shoreline plants are hardy and salt resistant, and the **hedges** that grow along the shore hardly exceed 5m (16ft). Some beautiful flowering plants like **bougainvillaea**, **red hibiscus** and frangipani have been cultivated. The **pink rose** is the Maldivian national flower.

In total the flora adds up to about 600 species, 100 of which can be said to have been on the islands before human occupation. With the settlers came 300 or so cultivated plants. Today fewer than 260 plant species are fully naturalized, meaning they have become part of the local plant life and grow freely in the wild. Part of this group are the pan-tropical weeds (weeds that commonly grow throughout the tropics) that accompany human activity. Five species of the genus *Pandanus*, the screwpine, occur nowhere else in the world.

The Animal Kingdom

In comparison to its marine counterpart, where coral species, reef fish and large, open water fish display an infinite array of colours, wildlife above the water is fairly sparse. Recently the government has shown growing concern for the environment. As a result, steps have been taken towards creating a National Environmental Council and sponsoring research and conservation work.

THE SMALLER CREATURES

- Look out for the beautiful **butterflies**. There are 67 species on the islands.
- Among the smaller creatures are rhinoceros beetles, paperwasps, mosquitoes and flies. Mosquitoes are the most common, although there is no danger of malaria.
- Small **scorpions** can inflict a harmless sting, and a large **centipede** gives a venomous, painful but not fatal bite.

RESIDENT HERONS

You are bound to see a heron on your resort island. There are about 13 species of heron that populate the islands, the most common being the **grey heron** (*Ardea cinerea rectirostris*), 'maakanaa' in Dhivehi. Most islands have a resident heron. They are quite used to people and make the most of the moment when tourists feed the fish off the jetty. Coming to the surface to snatch a piece of bread, the fish are easy prey as the heron waits for the right moment to impale a juvenile fish.

CHEEKY CROWS

The first mariners carried crows in cages aboard their ships when travelling over unknown seas. When they thought land was close by, they released the crows. The birds flew off directly towards land, if it was near, otherwise they hovered above, circling the ship and returning to the floating vessel.

The black **Indian house crow** (*Corvus splendens*), 'kaalhu' in Dhivehi, is now so common that it has become a pest. In the villages it steals drying fish and pecks valuable fruit from trees. On resort islands it perches near restaurants and bars, waiting for leftovers or handouts.

Large **flying foxes** or fruit bats (*Pteropus gigantues ariel*) hang from the branches of trees during the day and fly about at night, causing extensive damage to fruit trees. Two types of **gecko** (*Hemidactylus frenatus* and *Hemidactylus brookii*), 'hoanu' in Dhivehi, are found on the islands. These tiny creatures can be seen on walls at night near a bright light, their wide, unblinking eyes forever searching for moths and insects. Their surprisingly high-pitched 'bark' will probably be the last sound a tourist hears before falling asleep.

The garden **lizard** (*Calotes versicolor*), called 'bondu' in Dhivehi, is quite common and harmless, while a rapid-moving **skink** (*Riopa albopunctata*), 'garahita' in Dhivehi, is occasionally seen sunning itself during the day. Two species of harmless snake exist but are rarely seen: the small wolf snake (*Lycondon aulicus capucinus*) and the worm-like blind snake (*Typhlops braminus*).

Over 165 bird species have been identified in Maldives and at least 20 of these are actual residents. The **koel bird** (*Eudynamys scolopacea*) is often heard but rarely seen; the males have a shimmering black plumage with a bright green bill. The bright green, **rose-ringed parakeet** (*Psittacula krameri*) is common around Malé.

A unique bird to Maldives – the white-breasted **waterhen** (*Amaurornis phoenicurus maldivus*) – is common on the islands. The **lesser noddy** (*Anous tenuirostris*) and the **common noddy** (*Anous stolidus pileatus*) have become helpful guides for fishermen who search for schools of tuna.

HISTORY IN BRIEF

The origin of the first settlers of the Maldivian Archipelago, before their conversion to Islam, is obscure. Recent archaeological findings seem to suggest that the archipelago was inhabited as long ago as 1500BC.

The **Giraavaru** people, a close-knit community that's now almost extinct, claim to be the original inhabitants of the islands.

It seems almost certain that the first known inhabitants of Maldives came from **India** and **Ceylon** (present day Sri Lanka). Clues of this may be seen in the Buddhist customs that were practised before the conversion to Islam.

A few islands still have the remains of *stupas*: mounds of coral stone that resemble monuments found in the Buddhist capital of Sri Lanka. Relics discovered among the coral rag have distinct Buddhist characteristics.

Opposite: *The grey heron is the most common type of heron found on the islands.*

HISTORICAL CALENDAR

500BC Possibly the first settlers arrive on the islands.
AD1152 Conversion to Islam; start of the sultanate.
1558 The Maldivian nation enters a dark era under the Portuguese that lasts for approximately 15 years.
1573 Portuguese rule comes to an end after a successful Maldivian uprising.
1752 The Ali Rajas attack the archipelago, kidnap the sultan and take over the islands. Their victory is short-lived and after a few weeks the Maldivians gain their independence again.
1887 Maldives becomes a British protectorate.
1932 The first constitution is drawn but discarded in 1939.
1953 Maldives becomes a republic after abolishing the sultanate, but the country reverts back to the sultanate shortly afterwards.

1956 The British lease the island of Gan in the southernmost atoll of Seenu (Addu).
1957 Ibrahim Nasir is elected prime minister. He changes the conditions of the lease on Gan and demands that the British stop employing local labour.
1959 Objecting to Nasir's changes, the inhabitants of the three southernmost atolls protest against the government. They form the United Suvadive Islands and elect a president, Abdulla Afif Didi.
1962 Nasir dispatches gunboats to end the rebellion in the southern atolls. Afif Didi flees to Seychelles and the other leaders are banished to different islands.
1965 The British relinquish protectorate status. Maldives becomes independent.
1968 The second republic is formed with Ibrahim Nasir as president.

1972 The country is opened to tourism.
1974 On 24 June a crowd gathers to protest against the rising food prices. Nasir orders the police to open fire.
1978 Fearing for his life, Nasir retires to Singapore. Abdul Gayoom is elected the new president. He denounces Nasir's regime and banishes its corrupt members.
1980 An attempted coup against Gayoom fails and more people are banished including foreign mercenaries.
1988 Gayoom is re-elected for his third term of office. Local businessmen, aided by Sri Lankan mercenaries, try to overthrow the government. The National Security Service apprehend the perpetrators.
1993 Gayoom is elected for the fourth time.
2004 Gayoom remains the head of state.

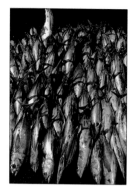

Above: *Since the 14th century, fishing has been an important source of trade and income for the Maldivian people.*
Opposite: *Initially the dominant religion, Buddhism was later replaced with Islam.*

CULTURAL CONTRASTS

Although locals work on tourist islands, and tourists may visit the fishing villages, the locals generally keep to their separate islands for two main reasons: many of the islands are too small to house both a tourist resort and a village and, secondly, the strict Islamic rule that governs Maldives prohibits the locals from consuming alcohol or pork. These are available to tourists on resort islands. Dogs are considered unhealthy pets and are not allowed on any of the islands. Nudity, drugs and firearms are also prohibited.

Some of the Buddhist temples that predate the Islamic conversion were destroyed in the ardour of the new-found religion, and others were covered and forgotten with time. Unfortunately, from the 1800s onwards, foreigners excavated the ancient sites and many were destroyed and plundered. Only in 1979 did the government start recognizing the historical value of the sites and a law was passed to protect them.

Foreign Travellers

Evidence found in travellers' writings and old sea charts seems to suggest that the country was a stopoff point for seafarers long before the Europeans took to conquering the seas. **Greeks**, **Romans**, **Egyptians**, **Phoenicians**, **Indonesians**, **Arabs** and **Africans** all landed on the tiny islands for fresh supplies.

The first known mention of the islands occurs between the 2nd and 6th centuries when travellers made fleeting references to the Maldivian Archipelago. From the 9th century Arab traders visited the area more frequently and left more detailed accounts.

A copy of the *Tarikh* was published by **H.C.P. Bell**, after he visited the islands several times between 1879 and 1922. Bell also published his own book: a chronicle of Maldivian history that offers a concise account of Maldivian life between the years of 1153 and 1821, after the conversion to Islam.

Ibn Battutah was a great **Moroccan** traveller who visited and stayed on the islands on several occasions during the 14th century. He wrote of the regular trade in fish, coconuts, coir, cowrie shells, tortoiseshell and ambergris (intestinal secretion of whales used in the manufacture of perfumes) that Maldivians had with **Arabia**, **India** and **China**. He also gave detailed accounts of the life and culture of the people.

In 1602 **François Pyrard**, a French sailor, was shipwrecked on the islands. He was kept captive on the islands for about five years until he finally managed to escape by boarding a passing foreign ship. His memoirs were published in 1619.

During the 1800s, British naval officers such as **Lieutenant Christopher** published their memoirs, giving their impressions of the Maldivian people and their customs. All these travellers wrote of a friendly yet reserved, honest and sincere race.

The Arabs and the Advent of Islam

As the Arabs spread their influence across the Indian Ocean and the Asian mainland, they recognized Maldives as being a perfect stopover to replenish their fresh water and food supplies. They also collected cowrie shells to trade for rice and slaves, and stayed on the islands long enough to marry a temporary wife – a sailor could easily repudiate her once he had to leave the country.

Conversion from **Buddhism** to **Islam** apparently occurred when **Abu al-Barakat Yusuf al-Barbari**, an Arab from North Africa, supposedly exorcised the monster that people believed was eating young virgins who had been offered in sacrifice. **Theemugey Maha Kaliminja**, the Buddhist ruler at the time (1153), was so impressed with Abu al-Barakat that he converted to Islam. It is said, by a few wise Maldivian men, that there never was a monster. They believe that the king had a perverted taste for young virgins and that when he was discovered by the Arabs, he promised to convert his whole country to Islam in return for the man's silence.

Kaliminja changed his name to **Sultan Dharmas Mohammed Ibn Abdullah** and began his 13-year reign as a Muslim during which time he built mosques and started practising justice according to Islamic law.

A political interpretation as to why the ruling elite adopted Islam differs from previous explanations: apparently Buddhist Sri Lanka was closing in on Maldives and in order to keep the Sri Lankans at arm's length, they would need as allies the powerful Islamic fleets that roamed the Indian Ocean. The ruling class benefited in other ways too: in becoming a Muslim country they became part

THE DYNASTIES OF THE SULTANATE

- **Theemuge Dynasty:** lasted 235 years with 26 rulers.
- **Hilali Dynasty:** lasted 170 years with 29 rulers. The last of the 29 Sultans, Ali VI, was made a martyr when he was killed while trying to defend his country against the invading Portuguese armies.
- **Utheem Dynasty:** lasted 127 years with 12 rulers. This dynasty was founded by Mohamed Thakurufanu the Great, who freed the country from the Portuguese.
- **Isdhoo Dynasty:** lasted five years with two rulers.
- **Dhiyamigili Dynasty:** lasted 55 years with three rulers.
- **Buraage Dynasty:** lasted 201 years with 13 rulers. The founder of this dynasty was Ghazi Hassan Izzuddeen, the leader of the local forces which repelled the Ali Rajas. After this dynasty the country became a Republic in 1968.

Below: *The tombstones of past rulers and important people lie here quietly amid the grounds of Friday Mosque which is one of the oldest and most exquisite mosques in Malé.*

of the Arab trading network, thus being able to exchange rare and luxury goods; and in following the strict Islamic code of law, the role of the central aristocracy was strengthened, making it easier to govern the widely scattered islands of the archipelago.

Early history is shrouded in mystery and legend and it is only recently that a new generation of historians has begun delving into the obscure past, hoping to find the true roots of their country.

The Sultanate

A lineage of sultans ruled the country from the conversion to Islam, beginning in 1153, to the declaration of a republic in 1968. Within this period there were brief intermissions of Portuguese and presidential rule. A total of 85 rulers, belonging to six different dynasties, succeeded each other.

The Portuguese

During the 16th century, Portuguese ships navigated the Indian Ocean and, realizing the strategic importance of Maldives, they attacked Malé. They killed the **Sultan, Ali VI**, and reinstated **Kalhu Mohammed** to the throne. A heartless and deceitful tyrant, he gave the Portuguese freedom over the islands. His successor, **Sultan Hasan IX**, was no better and he in turn offered the Portuguese complete control of the islands.

The Dutch and British

By the 17th century the Portuguese had lost their power in the Indian Ocean and the Dutch fleet took control. Maldives formed diplomatic ties with the Dutch and the trading relationship lasted for almost two centuries.

In 1796 the **Dutch** ceded Sri Lanka to the **British** and trade between Malé and Colombo thrived. By the mid-1800s, the extravagant and lazy Sultan had almost led his kingdom to bankruptcy and was forced to invite Indian **Borah merchants** to set up shops and trade. They became very successful and the locals eventually saw this as an attempt to take over their country, so they burnt down the Borah's shops and warehouses. The British governor intervened to keep the peace and guaranteed the Maldivians their independence provided the country became a British protectorate. In return the British pledged to protect the small island kingdom against enemies and not interfere in internal affairs. This relationship lasted until 1965 when the Maldives became independent.

There is also a second version of events: apparently, after Athirege Ameer Ibrahim Dhoshimeyna Kilegefaanu became prime minister in 1883 he asked for help from the British to regain his power. Eager to get a foothold in the Indian Ocean before the Germans, the British obliged. After a futile attempt to get the Sultan Mohammed Mueenudden and his followers to sign the papers that would have made Maldives a British protectorate, they forced him to do so at gunpoint on 16 December 1887.

Above: *Maumoon Abdul Gayoom has represented his people as president of the Maldives since 1978 when he was first elected to office.*

The 20th Century

Since the advent of Islam in Maldives, various unwritten constitutional principles based on customs and religion were accepted by the people. Only in 1932, under pressure from the British, was the sultan forced to draw up a constitution greatly limiting his powers. The constitution proved unsuitable and was discarded in 1939. Under a new constitution, in 1943, the sultan at the time was forced to abdicate, and Mohammed Amin Didi, the prime minister, assumed control of the government.

It was in 1953 that Maldives first became a republic. Didi was elected president but his term was short-lived; unhappy people protested against his ban on smoking and the shortage of food, forcing him to resign. The republic was then abolished and the controversial constitution once more discarded. It took another 15 years before the republic was proclaimed again. The autocratic Ibrahim Nasir was elected president of the second republic on 11 November 1968. Nasir was succeeded by a more open-minded **Maumoon Abdul Gayoom** in 1978.

THE ISLANDS OF WOMEN

Many legends have been told of the origin of the Maldivian people. It has even been said that Sinhalese women were the first people of the islands called *Mahiladipa* or the islands of women. The friendly women welcomed travellers and bore their children. The mix and diversity of their lovers may be seen today in the faces of the Maldivian people.

Right: *The crew of a local fishing boat (or* masdhoni*) hunt for tuna in the age-old fashion against a backdrop of Malé's dramatic modern skyline.*

GOVERNMENT AND ECONOMY

Each of the 200 inhabited islands is ruled by an island council whose members are the **island chief** (*Katheeb*) and one or more **deputy chiefs** (*Kuda Katheeb*). They are responsible for the local implementation of government policies, the maintenance of law and order and the management of nearby uninhabited islands. The island chief gives daily reports to the **atoll chief** (*Atholhu Verin*) – his superior, and administrative head of the second tier of the governmental structure. Nominated by the president, the atoll chief is responsible for the political and economic welfare of the atoll while a judge (*Gaazee*) presides over judicial and religious matters.

At the top of the administrative pyramid is the legislative body (citizens' *majlis*) made up of 50 members chosen from all the atolls and Malé, and eight elected by the president. The president is the religious and political leader of the country and has supreme authority. He is elected by the citizens' *majlis* every five years and is confirmed by the public through a national, democratic referendum.

Islamic Law (*Shari'ah*) is the accepted and practised basic law that dictates the country's code of conduct. Imprisonment and banishment to isolated islands are the two most common forms of punishment for perpetrators, although crime is not rife.

Maldivian economy reflects the islands' geographical situation, and with the fishing grounds being very much larger than the land mass, it is no wonder that fishing is such an important industry while agriculture plays a minor role. Economic growth and development is greatly boosted by revenue from tourism.

Fishing

Modernization, and the need for the development and improvement of the fishing industry, led the government to initiate a programme to mechanize fishing *dhonis*. By the end of the 1970s most of the fishing fleet was motorized. This has boosted the fishing industry as *dhonis* travel faster and further in search of fishing grounds, thereby tripling their annual catch.

Until 1971 Maldives exported most of its fish – boiled, smoked, dried skipjack and tuna to Sri Lanka. However, due to the foreign exchange crisis, Sri Lanka was forced to limit its imports and the Maldivian government began to look for new markets. Agreements were signed with foreign companies for the purchase of frozen fish. The fishermen rejoiced at the deal as it is far less time-consuming to prepare fish for the freezer than for drying.

During the next decade it became obvious that additional infrastructure was needed and the factory at **Felivaru** (Lhaviyani Atoll) was expanded.

A Marine Research Centre of the **Ministry of Fisheries, Agriculture and Marine Resources** was established in 1984 to carry out research, not only on the fishing possibilities of the country, but to gather information on the marine environment that is the underlying structure to the fragile existence of the islands.

Fishermen are respected members of the community and in recognition a national **Fishermen's Day** is held on 10 December every year.

FISH FOR LIFE

The preparation of fish caught by fishermen follows a **traditional** process: the fish is first gutted and beheaded; it is then boiled in fresh water for 15 minutes. The slow process of smoking is done over a charcoal fire in the kitchen and takes 24 hours. Chunks of **tuna** and **jackfish** are then laid out in the sun for four days to complete the curing process. As tough as leather, the dried fish lasts for months and is an effective way of curing the daily catch in an environment that had neither electricity nor refrigeration.

Below: *Every afternoon, fishing* dhonis *enter Malé's inner harbour to offload their catch to be sold at the market.*

Transport and Communications

Maldives established its own **shipping** line in 1966 with
two 2500-tonne vessels. Today the enlarged fleet of the
Maldives National Ship Management handles 95% of the
country's imports.

Malé's port offers limited facilities for ocean-going
shipping liners. The smaller ships pull up to the wharf
and their cargo is offloaded by cranes. The larger ones
wait in the waters that surround Malé while cargo *dhonis*
move frenetically to and from the port, offloading or
loading the larger vessels. Inter-island travelling is done
by motorized *dhonis*, float planes and large speedboats.
Many resort islands have their own small fleet of
motorized maritime transport to transfer holiday-makers
and guests.

Communication systems are international. All tourist
resorts and major islands have telephones and
facsimiles. Some resorts even have satellite television.

Agriculture

Most of the islands of Maldives are smaller than 1km²
(½ sq mile) with an average elevation of 1.6m (5ft) above
sea level. The soil, which is not very fertile, tends to have
a high alkaline level caused by excess calcium found in

Left: *A fruit stall at a market in Malé. Sweet bananas, papaya, mangoes, limes and star-apples are grown privately by individual families, the surplus of which is taken to the market.*

Opposite: *Seaplanes can land anywhere near an island and are one of the most popular modes of transport for tourists.*

the fragmented coral rock. The islands form a total land area of 298km² (115 sq miles) and of this only about 10% is suitable for some sort of agricultural venture.

As there are no mountains, streams or rivers, Maldivians rely on natural rainfall. Crops grown include **finger millet**, **Italian millet** and **maize**. **Taro**, **cassava** and **sweet potato** are cultivated all year round. Recently attempts have been made to encourage people to return to farming, rather than depending on imported goods such as rice and wheat.

Uninhabited islands, especially the ones adjacent to inhabited ones, are often leased to individuals or villages who become responsible for the maintenance of the island's vegetation, **coconut trees** and **timber**. Coconut production is the dominant agricultural activity and a large variety of local timber is grown for domestic use.

Watermelons are grown mainly on Thoddoo Island in the Alifu (Ari) Atoll. **Sweet bananas**, **papaya**, **mangoes**, **limes**, **star-apples** and **guavas** are grown within the compounds of each family's property together with a few vegetables. Some villagers keep **goats** and **chickens** although space is limited.

OLD AND NEW

The resort islands have become an important source of employment for Maldivian men. Here they learn new **skills** and **languages** as well as earning a regular salary to support their families who have been left behind in their home villages. Tourism has revived the traditional making of **handicrafts**, readily sold to foreigners. It has also encouraged the practice of **traditional dancing** which is regularly performed at the resorts, as part of the Maldivian culture.

Right: *Old trees in a school's playground provide a shady alternative!*

THE PEOPLE

Maldivians call themselves *Dhivehin* or 'Island People'. Particularly on the village islands, they form a small, very close-knit and disciplined **Muslim** society that has not yet reached a total population of 300,000 people.

Shy yet friendly, tolerant and respectful, Maldivians welcome the modern tourist as they welcomed, thousands of years ago, the seafaring foreigners that brought an harmonious blend of exotic features noticeable in their friendly faces today. As part of a totally Muslim country, Maldivian society is governed by strict **Islamic Law** and its religious beliefs.

Traditions and Culture

The family is the basic and most important unit of the society with the husband being the head of the household and the woman the homemaker. Women run the household in the absence of their partners who are often away fishing or working on resort islands. **Women** are highly regarded in this pure Muslim culture; they have greater influence in the major decision making of family matters and enjoy equal status in the workplace as the government has ensured that they are offered equal opportunities in employment, remuneration and promotions and have equal access to education and professional training.

The government provides each Maldivian family with a piece of land that measures approximately 15m (50ft) by 30m (100ft) on which to build a house. Walls are made from **coral** pieces held together by lime which they produce from burning coral slowly and for a long time. In addition, a stronger cement is made from blending ash, lime, charcoal and syrup made from coconut sap. But, realizing the detriment that has been caused to the **coral reefs** by removing blocks to build houses, the government has strongly discouraged the use of coral. **Bricks** are being imported for building purposes although this is very expensive.

Language

Close contact with the Arab world and the Indian mainland influenced and changed the original Maldivian language and script and has brought about a distinctive language which is known today as **Dhivehi**. The oldest form of written Dhivehi can be seen on ancient tombstones and engraved stone slabs found in old mosques. The language seems to be based on the archaic form of **Sinhala** which is spoken in **Sri Lanka**, and the ancient Maldivian script seen on tombstones and documents resembles the medieval Sinhala alphabet.

Thaana is the written script which developed after the overthrow of the Portuguese in the 16th century when Maldivians decided to revive their Islamic faith. The new script is written from right to left. It has 24 letters in its alphabet of which nine are actually Arabic numerals. Vowels are recognized by a dash drawn above or below the letter.

English is rapidly gaining importance as the official second language in Maldives, owing to the steady increase of tourism and foreign trade.

DANCING

Dancing is traditional, **Bodu Beru** being the most popular of the ritual dances performed by men and having its origins in the beating drums of **East Africa**. The song and the music start with a slow beat that builds to a crescendo as the story told by the singer unfolds. The dance reaches a climax of wild beating drums and frantic movements which sometimes cause the performers to enter a transient state. Women's dances are more subdued and some have the distinct influence of the Indian mainland. **Maafathi Neshun** is danced in national dress. **Bandiyaa Jehun** is an adaptation of the Indian pot dance in which young women beat the rhythm of their music on their metal water pots.

Below: *Coconuts form part of the Maldivians' daily meals. Almost every part of it is used and the waste burnt.*

MARRIAGE AND DIVORCE

True to Muslim tradition, men may marry up to four wives, although in the current economic situation, very few can afford to support more than one. Maldives once had the reputation of having one of the highest divorce rates in the world. However, a new Family Law introduced in 2001 raised the age of marriage to 18 and made unilateral divorce illegal. A man can no longer divorce his wife by just telling her that she is divorced from him – both parties must now go through the courts. A divorce can only take place when all attempts at reconciliation have failed.

THE FIVE PILLARS OF ISLAM

• *Shahada* is the declaration of the Islamic faith that 'There is no God but Allah, and Mohammed is his prophet'.
• *Salath* or *namadh* is the call to prayer. All Muslims must pray five times a day facing Mecca.
• *Zakat* is the act of giving charity to the needy.
• *Ramadan* is the ninth month of the Islamic calendar. During this period all Muslims must fast during the day.
• *Haj* is the pilgrimage to Mecca that should be done at least once in the lifetime of every Muslim.

Religion

Islam is the only religion of the Maldives but the people have combined their own traditions with **Islam**, giving it its own character. Faith in Islam is taken very seriously and the law allows no deviations, especially regarding drinking alcohol or eating pork. Despite their piety, some Muslims are still very superstitious, believing in supernatural beings, among others *dhevi* or *jinni*.

Sport and Recreation

Locals are quick to consent to a game of volleyball or football played by tourists on the resort islands. Since a former sultan had insisted on building a football pitch on every island, the inter-atoll championship is taken very seriously. Less popular, **cricket** is played on Malé.

On the fishing islands, older men often play **cards** or **chess** and children play **Arabic board games**. Young girls always play *bashi*, an outdoor game considered to be a mixture of cricket and tennis.

Food and Drink

It comes as no surprise that the dietary content of the average Maldivian is **fish** and **coconuts**. This simple mixture is added to imported rice and spiced up with a curry paste made from **curry powder**, **lime**, **chilli** and

grated coconut. In the mornings the women make *roshi*, unleavened bread, and prepare fish broth, *garudia*, to be eaten with rice for the evening meal. Dried fish is made for home consumption and for export.

Luscious tropical fruits and vegetables are scarce. Locals do grow small quantities for their own consumption, but the soil is poor. They certainly could not supply the resort islands with fresh produce.

Resort islands import almost all the food they serve to tourists. Clever chefs can create sumptuous meals with the occasionally poor supplies of fresh produce. On the cheapest resorts and those furthest from Malé, a basic meal of tuna fish, tinned fruit, jelly and longlife milk often leads to complaints from tourists who are ignorant of the situation. Understand the circumstances and expect meat and chicken only occasionally, coloured cabbage and the tiny, sweet, local bananas that may be the only fresh fruit served. The five-star resorts serve excellent food but you pay for the privilege.

Muslims are not allowed alcohol and Maldivians generally drink very sweet tea, but resort islands do sell alcohol to all non-Muslims.

> ### SHORT EATS
>
> 'Short eats' are Maldivian **snacks** to whet your appetite between meals. You may savour the eats at teashops in Malé or at a Maldivian buffet organized on the resort islands on a traditional evening. Savoury 'short eats' are made with smoked tuna, coconut, lime juice, chopped onion and chilli. Sweet 'short eats' are made with flour, sugar, egg and coconut.

Opposite: *Islam is the official religion in the Maldives. All inhabited islands have at least one mosque.*
Left: *In her dark kitchen a woman prepares the rice for the evening meal. Her stove is a coal fire which she expertly keeps at a constant temperature convenient for cooking.*

2
Malé and Hulhule

Rising from a coral bed and only a few metres above sea level, **Malé** is a city that seems to float on water. Buildings meet the surrounding breakwaters and the port is so busy, one cannot see where the wharf begins or where the tightly-packed, floating vessels align.

Malé started off as one of the inhabited islands of the country, with a few thatched huts set among the tropical vegetation and the coconut palm trees. Because of its strategic position in the centre of the chain of 26 atolls that make up the Maldivian Archipelago, it soon became the seat of the sultanate and has retained its post as the capital city ever since.

Today it is the political, cultural and economic centre of the country. British mariners who visited the capital 50 years earlier referred to it as a 'sleepy village' in their writings. They would not recognize the bustling, major port city today with its clean, paved coral streets, beautifully kept, whitewashed coral houses, boulevards of busy shops, high-rise office blocks and throng of traffic.

The best way to get around the 1.6km² (1 sq mile) island is on foot. It takes about 30 minutes to cross its length, less than two hours to walk the perimeter, or you can hire an air-conditioned taxi. Bicycles – the most popular mode of transport with the inhabitants – are also an option. If you decide to hire one, you will quickly learn the rules of the road: ride where you find a gap! Bicycles, motorbikes, cars, trucks and pedestrians mingle in a confusion of legs, wheels and tyres.

INDIAN OCEAN

North Malé Atoll
(Kaafu Atoll)

Hulhule
Malé

South Malé Atoll
(Kaafu Atoll)

DON'T MISS

*** Islamic Centre and **Grand Friday Mosque:** the heart of the city.
*** Singapore Bazaar: to bargain for souvenirs.
** The Fish Market: where fishermen arrive in the afternoon to sell their catch.
** Friday Mosque, *Hukuru Miskiiy:* the oldest mosque in Malé, built in 1656.
* Sultan Park and **National Museum:** includes items from pre-Muslim civilizations.

Opposite: *The Jumhooree Maiden, in front of the inner harbour has become a popular meeting place.*

Right: *Fishing* dhonis *bring in their catch to the market in the afternoon. The boats are lined up along the pier while the fishermen offload skipjack and tuna.* **Opposite:** *Steps have been taken to accommodate the swelling population of Malé. Land has been reclaimed on the southern and western sides of the island and a port has been built to take the overflow of vessels that crowd the inner harbour.*

A GROWING CITY

Just over 1.6km² (1 sq mile) in size, one could barely call **Malé** a city, yet it is the heart of Maldives. From an island village, it has expanded through land reclamation into a well-organized city with over 70,000 inhabitants. High-rise buildings alleviate the demand for more space and wide roads cope with the concentrated traffic.

And for a nerve-shattering experience, ask one of the locals for a tour on the back of a scooter! As you venture into the outskirts of the island the frenetic pace slows down. Old men sit under large trees playing board games in front of mosques, while women collect water at the communal freshwater fountains if their houses do not have running water.

Malé is the crossroads for many people who come to the archipelago. It is the centre of Maldivian trading and for many local islanders it is their only contact with the outside world. But, as the fishing islands depend on Malé for trade and administration, the capital city depends on the fishing villages for its livelihood.

The markets are teeming with traders who come to buy and sell their goods. And since modernity has thrust itself onto this tiny capital, it has attracted the youth of the country, representing one-third of about 75,000 inhabitants. Steps have been taken to accommodate the swelling population by reclaiming land from the shallow waters between the island and its western and southern surrounding reefs. Traditional coral houses have been replaced by multistorey brick buildings to accommodate the growing population.

PLACES OF INTEREST

Arriving by *dhoni* from the airport, 10 minutes away, you will land in the inner harbour among cargo and fishing vessels. The waterfront has been divided into sections to accommodate the various cargo carried by the *dhonis* and other boats– passengers, fish or imports. The enclosing coral wall of the north inner harbour, with

its narrow entrance, was built between 1620 and 1648. Today a new harbour on the south side of the island has been built in an attempt to cope with the congestion of the older harbour with its many small cafés and shops.

SUBURBS OF MALÉ

Henveiru, situated in the northeastern section, includes the government offices, the waterfront and beautiful homes along Ameer Ahmed Magu (street). **Maafannu**, situated to the northwest, includes the president's residence and a few embassies. **Galolhu** is a small, tightly packed residential section of the city where narrow streets are lined with small houses. **Machchangolhi** includes the south end, the centre of the city and much of Malé's largest street, Majeedi Magu.

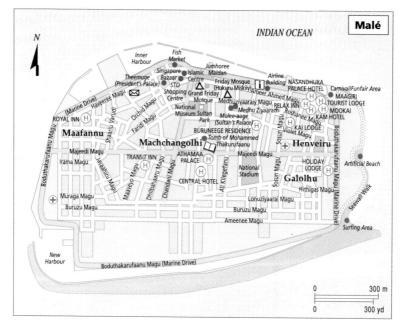

Malé

Below: *Outside the covered market, men sit and talk while others sell their goods of bananas and coconuts.*

Jumhooree Maiden **

The imposing and solitary wooden jetty along the wharf is the official arrival place for dignitaries; it heads the public park called **Jumhooree Maiden**. The new park was created in 1988 and has become a popular meeting place for both locals and tourists, who relax under the shade waiting for their groups to reunite. At night the youngsters gather here to hang out. On the eastern side of the park, on its permanent flag post, the Maldivian flag unfolds its colours in the gentle breeze.

Chandani Magu ***

Following **Marine Drive** west of **Jumhooree Maiden** you will come to the trading centre of Malé, the area where all the local markets are situated. Another street that runs into town from the west end of Jumhooree Maiden, **Chandani Magu**, has become the main area for souvenir shops. If you follow a guide he will take you to a relative's shop which may not necessarily mean it is the best in the street.

The Markets **

The **fish market** bustles with action in the afternoons as fishermen lay their catch on the shiny concrete slabs and barter with their customers. The incoming fishing *dhonis* are a fascinating sight for any onlooker. Fishermen fight

for space along the wharf, then pull back a tightly woven net to uncover their neatly stacked, tails-up catch. As a crew member freshens the fish by throwing buckets of water over the catch, the others rush to display their cargo on the market floor. Traditionally, no women are seen in the fish market as the catching, selling and buying of fish is considered a man's job.

Left: *The mosque's grand gold dome and towering minaret dominate the Malé skyline.*

Further down Marine Drive, at the **covered market**, locals buy commodities such as eggs, coconuts, spices, fruit and vegetables. Outside, in an open area under a huge leafy tree, men sit and talk while others sell wood brought to the market from neighbouring islands.

Islamic Centre ★★★

The new **Islamic Centre** located on **Ibraahimee Magu** houses the **Grand Friday Mosque** with its towering minaret. The centre's glittering gold dome, made of anodized aluminium, dominates the Malé skyline and is easily spotted from the sea and air. Opened on 11 November 1984, it is named after the national hero, Sultan Mohammed Thakurufanu Al A'z'am and displays beautiful wooden carvings with Arabic calligraphy done by local craftsmen. The

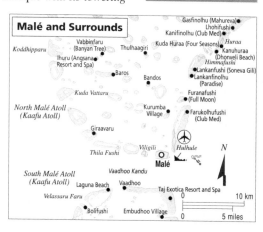

Malé and Surrounds

Gasfinolhu (Mahureva)
Lhohifushi
Kanifinolhu (Club Med)
Koddhippparu
Vabbinfaru (Banyan Tree)
Thulhaagiri
Kuda Huraa (Four Seasons)
Huraa
Kanuhuraa
Ihuru (Angsana) Resort and Spa
(Dhonveli Beach)
Himmafushi
Baros
Bandos
Lankanfushi (Soneva Gili)
Lankanfinolhu (Paradise)
Kuda Vattaru
Furanafushi (Full Moon)
North Malé Atoll (Kaafu Atoll)
Kurumba Village
Farukolhufushi (Club Med)
Giraavaru
Thila Fushi
Viligili
Hulhule
Malé
South Malé Atoll (Kaafu Atoll)
Vaadhoo Kandu
Laguna Beach
Vaadhoo
Velassaru Faru
Taj Exotica Resort and Spa
Bolifushi
Embudhoo Village

N
0   10 km
0   5 miles

mosque easily accommodates about 5000 devotees. The rest of the three-storey complex includes an Islamic library, a conference hall and classrooms. The imposing structure is flanked by the 40m-high (133ft) minaret.

Friday Mosque **

The oldest and most beautiful mosque in Malé is **Friday Mosque,** or **Hukuru Miskiiy**, located on Medhuziyaaraiy Magu. It was built in 1656 in coral rag and has been intricately carved with Arabic writings and ornamental patterns on the outside and inside. Wooden plates found in the mosque bear detailed accounts of the conversion of Maldivians to Islam. The mosque is set in a beautifully maintained garden with miniature gravelled pathways and a fountain.

The grounds also include a graveyard with carved tombstones of past rulers and important people. Gravestones with a rounded top indicate women's graves and those with a pointed top, men's graves.

The old minaret, **Munnaaru**, is close to the mosque.

Built in 1675, it was used five times a day as the voice of the *muezzin* rang out, calling worshippers to prayer. It now stands silent as its function has been taken over by the new, taller minaret of the Islamic Centre (*see* p. 31).

Sultan Park *

On the opposite side of the street, near Friday Mosque, is **Sultan Park**, a public park and a quiet oasis in the heart of the busy capital city. Originally the grounds of a palace, *Mulee-aage* was built in 1913 by Sultan Mohammed Shamsuddeen III in honour of his son, heir to the throne. Unfortunately, the Sultan was deposed and his son never inherited the royal position.

In 1953 the country became a republic for the first time and the colonial-looking building was altered, renamed the **Presidential Palace**, and used by the government as offices.

The short-lived republic was replaced once more by the sultanate which was finally abolished in 1968. After the second republic was formed, the Sultan's Palace was demolished except for one three-storey wing that was converted to the National Museum.

The National Museum *

Artefacts housed in the building include pre-Islamic stone objects donated by members of the island communities or found during archaeological diggings, and regal costumes worn by kings and queens. Furniture and armaments of past royalty, photographs of important personalities and manuscripts with famous inscriptions take you on a swift journey through Maldivian culture and tradition. Look out for the coral stone carving of Buddha and a wooden panel inscribed in Arabic which was transferred from Friday Mosque.

Memorials

The **Tomb of Mohammed Thakurufanu** located in Neeloafaru Magu is dedicated to the Maldivian hero who defeated the Portuguese invaders in the 16th century (1573) and restored independence to the country.

Sultan Ali VI is remembered in the **Ali Rasgefaanu Ziyaaraiy Memorial** situated in Maafannu, Shaheed Ali Higun. The memorial marks the spot where the sultan fell while fighting the Portuguese in 1558.

The sultan reigned for about two and a half months before he was killed. His memorial was situated on the beach but recent reclamation of land has pushed it further inland (*see* p. 15).

Although he was not a war hero, the memorial to Abu al-Barakat Yusuf al-Barbari, **Medhu Ziyaarath**, in Medhuziyaaraiy Magu is a shrine dedicated to the man who was supposedly responsible for the country's conversion to Islam (*see* p. 14).

Above: *The beautiful Hukuru Miskiiy, Malé's oldest mosque, was built in 1656 and is decorated with intricately carved Arabic writing and patterns.* **Opposite:** *The Grand Friday Mosque and Islamic Centre were opened in 1984. The mosque can accommodate some 5000 worshippers while the rest of the building offers a library, a conference hall and classrooms.*

Right: *The Tomb of Mohammed Thakurufanu honors the memory of the Maldivian hero who defeated the Portuguese invaders.*
Below: *Malé street scene. The capital island is a thriving centre with brightly coloured new buildings thrusting skywards.*

Where to Eat in Malé

To further experience Malé, you should finish your tour in one of the many **teashops** that offer freshly

brewed tea, short eats (*see* p. 25 and At a Glance p. 37) and spicy curries, or one of the **restaurants** that specialize in Oriental, Asian, Italian or European delicacies. A few names to remember are Lighthouse Café, Ocean Café, Relax Inn, Salsa Royal, Symphony, Tandoor, Thai Wok, Trends and West Park Restaurant. None are licensed as Malé is a Muslim city and it is forbidden to consume alcohol.

HULHULE

When flying towards Malé, you should spot the city from the air as a speck in the ocean with no space for a runway. As the plane starts descending, you may be inclined to think that the pilot has made a mistake and is about to plunge the whole plane load of passengers into the warm, inviting waters of the tropical sea . . . when suddenly, the plane touches down on firm ground!

Hulhule International Airport

Airport related facilities, including those for National transfers, are the only buildings found on this **island**, 4km (2.5 miles) from Malé and the runway is the only one in the world that begins and ends in the sea.

During the rule of the sultanate, Hulhule was an exclusive retreat for the sultan, his family and friends. The island would be unrecognizable to those nobles who once used it for their pleasure. A major part of it is now covered by tarmac as the runway stretches south to north from breakwater to breakwater.

The first jet landed in 1977 and the new International Airport with its extended runway was opened in 1981. The recently renovated terminal building has also been extended in order to accommodate the ever-increasing flow of tourists and businessmen. It contains reasonably priced duty-free shops some of which even sell chocolate, crisps, cooldrinks – and beer. at the entrance to the building there is a well-stocked souvenir shop for some last-minute shopping, but be warned, prices here are certainly no bargain.

ACCOMMODATION

Maldives is one of the poorest countries in the world but the people are warm and friendly and very hospitable, and provide the best they can under the circumstances. Many of the guesthouses cannot provide the standard of service tourists from first world countries expect. The **hotels** in Malé may be more expensive than the guesthouses but at least you will be guaranteed good service, adequate facilities, private bathrooms and hot and cold, freshwater showers. **Guesthouses** vary in range from tiny and modest abodes to spacious rooms. They do not offer hot or fresh water but some of the better ones have air conditioning. You may find that you have to share your room as well as the bathroom with strangers. If you decide on this option, it is advisable to bring your own sheeting.

Left: *Aerial view of Malé (the completely built-up capital island, on the right) and Hulhule (the airport island, on the left).*

WHAT TO BUY

- **Lacquer work:** delicately carved wooden pots, boxes and vases decorated in red, black and yellow resin.
- **Printed T-shirts** and **handmade clothing:** choose your own design and the T-shirt is yours as soon as the dye dries. Clever tailors can make a dress or a pair of shorts in your chosen fabric in a few hours.
- **Beautiful handcrafted jewellery:** made from imported gold and silver.
- **Souvenirs** and **trinkets:** created from coconut shells and **baskets** made from woven palm leaves.
- **Mats** (*kuuna*): woven from thin rushes in different colours and geometric designs.
- **Cotton sarongs:** woven with brown and black strands.

Below: Dhonis *and speed-boats transfer the tourists to their resorts.*

The Satellite Restaurant, which is adjacent to the terminal building, offers a variety of meals in a comfortable air conditioned waiting area on the inside, with tables and chairs in the shade of a few trees just outside.

Transfers to Resort Islands

Once you have passed through customs, you proceed to the arrivals area. Here, under a long tin roof cover, island representatives await your arrival. Outside the airway terminal, a long, covered walkway leads to several jetties reserved for vessels taking tourists to their holiday destinations.

Seaplanes take off from the opposite side of the island on their way to the furthermost islands. Your package deal should clearly stipulate whether your transfer is by boat, speedboat or seaplane. **Water taxis** to Malé are available for the short 10-minute ride to the capital city.

Hulule Island Hotel

An 88-bed luxury hotel with excellent restaurant and café. The delightful swimming pool area and bars are popular with the ex pats. There is a complimentary shuttle to Malé for guests.

Malé and Hulhule at a Glance

Clear skies and calm seas in the dry monsoon months (**Nov– Apr**), tropical showers in the wet months (**May–Oct**).

International flights land at **Hulhule** International Airport. A few visitors arrive on ships that sail between Colombo (Sri Lanka) and Maldives.

Regular taxi *dhonis* between **Hulhule** and **Malé**. In the city, walking is best (it takes about 30 minutes to cross the island). There are taxis and bicycles on Malé. Package tours include airfare, transfers to islands, accommodation and meals.

HIGH-RANGE
Hulule Island Hotel, tel: 33-0888, fax: 33-0777.
Kam Hotel, Meheli Goalhi, tel: 32-0611, fax: 32-0614. Japanese-like garden.
Mookai Hotel, tel: 33-8811, fax: 33-8822. Modern rooms, pool, sauna, gym; sea views.
Nasandhura Palace Hotel, Boduthakurufaanu Magu, tel: 32-3380, fax: 32-0822. Near harbour; modern facilities.
Relax Inn, Ameeru Ahmed Magu, tel: 31-4531/2, fax: 31-4533. Sea views.

MID-RANGE
Buruneege Residence, Hithaffinvaa Magu, tel: 33-0011, fax: 33-0022. Simple rooms, basic facilities; restaurant.
Central Hotel, Rahdhebai Magu, tel: 31-7766, fax: 31-5383. Central with all facilities.
Kai Lodge, Violet Magu, tel: 32-8742.
Maagiri Tourist Lodge, Boduthakurufaanu Magu, Henveiru, tel: 32-2576, fax: 32-8787. Air conditioned.
Transit Inn, Maveyo Magu, tel: 32-0420, fax: 32-9665. In quiet street. Cold showers.

Al Fresco Café, STO shopping complex. Burgers, curries and local short eats. Popular.
Carnival site, variety of restaurants, some with sea views.
Esjehi Gallery Café, Medhuziyaaraiy Magu. Coffees, light snacks. Set in the garden of an old-style Maldivian house.
Farivalhu Restaurant, at Central Hotel, tel: 31-7766. International cuisine; Asian; seafood and fish and chips.
Kam Hotel Restaurant, at Kam Hotel (*see* Where to Stay), tel: 32-0611, fax: 32-0614. Open breakfast till late.
Lighthouse Café, G.Zafna, Lily Magu, tel: 31-0900. Good food; reasonably priced.
Mövenpick, popular open-air ice-cream parlour on east coast; artificial beach.
Ocean Café, Boduthakuru Magu, tel: 33-2707. Overlooks ocean; partly open air; international cuisine; good value.
Salsa Royal, Orchid Magu, tel: 33-5008. Smart Italian style eaterie popular with locals.
Satellite Restaurant, at the airport. Continental, Italian, German and Asian fare including hotdogs, seafood, pizzas.
Seagull Café House, 2 Fareedhee Magu, tel: 32-3792. Italian and continental. Famous for its ice creams.
Shell Beans, on Boduthakurufaanu Magu overlooking port. Sandwiches and pastries.
Symphony, Athana Goalhi, tel: 32 62 77. Well established and popular.
Tandoor, pizza hut; open-air seating; artificial beach.
Thai Wok, Ameer Ahmed Magu, tel: 31-0007. Traditional Thai favourites in pleasant ambience.
Trends, at Nasandhura Palace Hotel (*see* Where to Stay), tel: 32-3380. Good food; a lovely garden setting.
West Park Restaurant, tel: 31-6954. Pleasant setting overlooks sea on the NW corner. Reasonably priced.
Teashops throughout the island offer drinks, local specialities and eats at cheap prices.

Fishing safaris and speedboat excursions can be arranged (*see* Travel Tips). Most resorts arrange diving and snorkelling safaris, island-hopping excursions and trips to local villages. Shopping trips to Malé are also available.

Maldives Tourism Promotion Board, *see* page 47.

3
Central and
Southern Atolls

For practical purposes the Maldivian atolls have been grouped into **five sections** in this guide. The central atolls are the most frequented by foreigners and include the capital city, Malé, the heart of Maldivian economy. Next to Malé, Hulhule International Airport is the link to the outside world. And, scattered among the islands of the atolls closest to the airport, are the resort islands. They serve as a mecca for over 500,000 tourists who come every year to soak up the sun, enjoy the tropical beauty and discover the country's marine treasures.

The central section includes the three atolls of **Kaafu** (North and South Malé), **Ari** (Alifu) and **Felidhu** (Vaavu); the most popular holiday destinations because of the concentration of resort islands. These sections are covered under separate chapters (*see* p. 59–104).

Of the other **five central atolls** that stretch south from the three resort-filled ones, **Meemu** (Mulaku), **Faafu** (North Nilandhoo) and **Dhaalu** (South Nilandhoo) have recently been designated by the Government as part of the tourist zone and a total of five new resort islands have been developed in these atolls. The remaining atolls **Thaa** (Kolhumadulu) and **Laamu** (Hadhdhunmathi) are not within the tourist area and rarely see foreign visitors.

At first glance, fishing villages may all seem the same, but venture into them, talk to the locals and you will discover clever craftsmen, regal tombs aged by many years under the sun, treasures hidden under Buddhist mounts (*hawittas*), and nesting turtles.

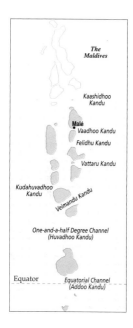

Opposite: *Most inter-island travel is done aboard colourful* dhoni *boats. These slow-moving local vessels offer tourists a leisurely sea ride.*

Right: *Most Maldivian life takes place outdoors. While these children's mother is weaving a new mat, her young daughter feeds and looks after the toddler.*

ATOLL FACTS AND FIGURES

Kaafu (North Malé and South Malé) Total population (excluding Malé) 11,650; population of Malé over 70,000; 44 resorts; capital Thulusdhoo.

Ari (Alifu) Total population 11,744; some 60 uninhabited islands; 29 resorts; capitals Mahibadhoo and Rasdhoo.

Vaavu (Felidhu) Total population 1779; 2 resorts; capital Felidhoo.

Meemu (Mulaku) Total population 5000; about 23 uninhabited islands; 2 resorts; capital Muli.

Faafu (North Nilandhoo) Total population 3800; 1 resort; capital Magoodhoo.

Dhaalu (South Nilandhoo) Total population 5000; 2 resorts, capital Kudahuvadhoo.

Thaa (Kolhumadulu) Total population 9300; no resorts; capital Veymandoo.

Laamu (Hadhdhunmathi) Total population 11,600; no resorts; capital Hithadhoo.

The **Southern** administrative atolls of **Gaafu Alifu** (North Huvadhoo), **Gaafu Dhaalu** (South Huvadhoo), **Gnaviyani** (Foammulah) and **Seenu** (Addu) are separated from the central atolls by the **One-and-a-Half-Degree Channel** (Huvadhoo Kandu) that gets its name from its longitude. The channel is also very wide, almost 100km (60 miles), and 2066m (6780ft) deep. Past the channel, the southern atolls are fairly isolated from the rest of the archipelago as they stretch down over the equator. They may be detached from the heart of Maldives, but these three atolls have not been forgotten. Strategically placed on the main sea route to India, they have received the greatest score of foreign contingencies throughout the centuries, and have the archaeological sites to prove it. They have developed their own trading ties with Sri Lanka, rather than with Malé.

The great expanse of water that separate them, not only from the rest of the islands but from one another as well, has been conducive to the individual development of each atoll on its own. The dialect of the different atolls varies from one to another and from the general Maldivian spoken language. Luxuriating in lush vegetation and with a climate that promotes a healthy crop, the atolls are largely self-sufficient.

THE CENTRAL ATOLLS
Meemu (Mulaku) Atoll

Meemu is about 120km (75 miles) from Malé and its capital, **Muli**, is the atoll's main fishing centre with its nine fishing islands located on the east side. There are two resort islands in Meemu Atoll: the long, narrow island of **Medhufushi** offers a high standard of accommodation and good facilities. There are 120 rooms including water bungalows and suites all with air conditioning and hot and cold water. **Hakuraa Club** has just over 70 water bungalows and 10 beach bungalows. The island has a very large shallow lagoon on the west side.

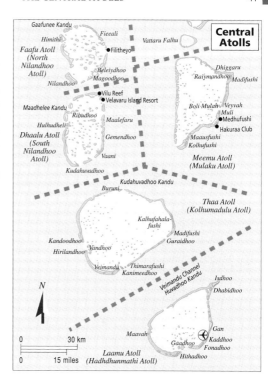

Faafu (North Nilandhoo) Atoll

Faafu is the true central atoll of Maldives. Its strategic situation has drawn religious settlers to its coral islands, a base from which they intended spreading their teachings to the rest of the Maldivian population. **Nilandhoo** is the site of one of the most important archaeological finds in Maldives. A vast temple complex of possibly Hindu origin was found buried under the second-oldest mosque of the country. The dressed stones of the ancient temple were used in AD1153 to build the mosque. Inside *Aasaari Miskiiy* (mosque), the walls are heavily decorated with Arabic carvings. Located on the east side of the atoll, **Filitheyo Island Resort** is 120km from the airport and provides accommodation in 125 bungalows some of which are built on stilts over the water.

JEWELLERS

The large concentration of jewellers on the islands of **Dhaalu Atoll** came about centuries ago when the sultan banished his chief jeweller to the island of **Rinbudhoo**. The sultan had given his jeweller gold to make jewellery but instead, the jeweller was caught using gold-plated silver. The exiled craftsman taught his skills to the islanders, who have passed the art on from generation to generation.

Dhaalu (South Nilandhoo) Atoll

Dhaalu Atoll is 160km (100 miles) from the capital city of Malé, just below Faafu (North Nilandhoo Atoll) and has eight fishing islands and around 40 uninhabited islands. The capital island is Kudahuvadhoo and here the archaeologist Thor Heyerdahl excavated a number of sites. The islands on the northern rim of the atoll have the reputation of having the finest jewellery makers in the Maldives.

Two tourist resorts have been developed on the northeast side of the atoll. **Vilu Reef Beach and Spa Resort**, situated 128km (75 miles) from Malé, is a tiny island offering an excellent standard of accommodation in just 68 thatched rooms. The resort has a tennis court and a good range of water-sports facilities. **Velavaru Island Resort** has 66 semi-detached and 18 individual thatched bungalows, a restaurant, bar, spa, diving school and water-sports center.

Thaa (Kolhumadulu) Atoll

Thaa Atoll, about 190km (120 miles) from Hulhule International Airport, lies south of Meemu and Dhaalu atolls across the **Kudahuvadhoo Channel**. Hidden among the lush vegetation there are remains of old sultans' residences and their tombs; and buried under many centuries of accumulated sand, *hawittas* bear testament to the country's pre-Islamic culture. **Fahala**, on the atoll's eastern side, is one of the largest uninhabited islands in the group.

Laamu (Hadhdhunmathi) Atoll

The southernmost atoll of the central group is separated from Thaa Atoll by **Veimandu Channel** (**Hadhdoo Kadu**) which is 26km (16 miles) wide and 2044m (6708ft) deep. It is 225km (140 miles) from the international airport and has no resorts. The atoll has a small airport on the island of **Kadhdhoo**. Laamu's islands have been inhabited for many thousands of years. The remains of a thriving Buddhist sect have been found on **Maabaidhoo**, **Mundoo** and **Gan**. More recent relics of the past are two wrecks that ran aground on the encircling atoll reefs: the French *François* in 1873 and the British *Lagan Bank* which sunk off the northern tip of the atoll in 1938.

Above: *Dharanboodhoo beaches are a favourite nesting ground for turtles.*

THE SOUTHERN ATOLLS
Gaafu Alifu (North Huvadhoo) Atoll

Huvadhoo is one of the world's largest atolls and, because of its size, it has been split into two (Gaafu Alifu and Gaafu Dhaalu) for administrative purposes. Almost round, with a northerly protrusion, the entire atoll measures 70km (43 miles) from north to south and 55km (34 miles) across, enclosing a lagoon that covers 2240km^2 (870 sq miles) and reaching a depth of almost 90m (300ft). The atoll's islands support a population of about 20,000.

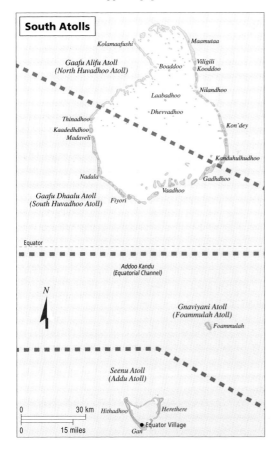

South Atolls

Kolamaafushi
Maamutaa

Gaafu Alifu Atoll
(North Huvadhoo Atoll)
Boaddoo
Viligili
Kooddoo

Laabadhoo
Nilandhoo

Dhevvadhoo

Thinadhoo
Kaadedhdhoo
Madaveli
Kon'dey

Kanduhulhudhoo

Nadala
Gadhdhoo

Gaafu Dhaalu Atoll
(South Huvadhoo Atoll)
Vaadhoo
Fiyori

Equator

Addoo Kandu
(Equatorial Channel)

N

Gnaviyani Atoll
(Foammulah Atoll)
Foammulah

Seenu Atoll
(Addu Atoll)

0   30 km   Hithadhoo   Herethere
0   15 miles   Equator Village
                     Gan

THE ISLAND OF TURTLES

Dharanboodhoo's beaches on Faafu Atoll have always been the favoured nesting areas for turtles. At night, during the southwest monsoon (Apr–Oct), they swim to the beach to lay their eggs. The turtles hide the eggs under beach vegetation, but unfortunately too many of the eggs have landed on the islanders' table. Many of these reptiles have been killed for the adornment of tourists. This has created an alarming decline in the turtle population. Today, many projects have been developed to try to save these harmless reptiles. Hopefully we will see a greater awareness among the locals and a better appreciation for turtles from the tourist.

A STRAINED RELATIONSHIP

The strained relationship between the southern atolls and their northern counterparts, worsened between the 1950s and 1960s when the government stopped the southern fishermen from trading their catch with Colombo merchants. Islanders were also forbidden to be employed by the British staging post that had been established on Gan. Conflict was inevitable. The three southern atolls broke away and formed the United Suradive Islands, but their independence was short-lived. Today the Maldivian government encourages the development of the southern atolls, promoting foreign investment.

THE KINGDOM OF CATS

The small island of **Gadhdhoo** houses a population of over 2000 people; and yet no families will move onto the neighbouring island of **Gan**, which is bigger and uninhabited. The islanders only use Gan as an Islamic cemetery. Staunch in their beliefs, the islanders take a local legend seriously and will not inhabit the forsaken island which has come to be known as the 'Kingdom of Cats'. The legend describes the invasion of the island by big cats that killed and chased away the local inhabitants. The historical explanation is that the island was probably invaded by **Sinhalese** people from **Sri Lanka** who called themselves '**Lion People**' and wore ugly, feline masks for ceremonial purposes. As the islanders were probably Hindu at the time, and the invaders Buddhist, it was more than likely a religious conflict.

Gaafu Alifu is the northern administrative section of the large atoll. It is 330km (205 miles) from Malé. *Hawittas* and unexplored ruins lie in the thickets of the islands, while on **Kon'dey** an archaeologist discovered the limestone sculpture of a Hindu water god.

In line with the main shipping route, the atoll has claimed some wrecks: The *Surat* in 1800 and, more recently, the *Nicolaos Embricos* that sank in 1969.

Gaafu Dhaalu (South Huvadhoo) Atoll

The southern section of Huvadhoo Atoll is 360km (223 miles) from Malé. In 1993 a new regional airport was opened on **Kaadedhdhoo**, linking the atoll to the capital by air.

The islands that stretch along the southern rim of the atoll are littered with ancient ruins and artefacts dating back to Hindu and Buddhist times. Deep in the jungle of the uninhabited island of **Gan** are the remains of a pyramid that probably dominated the island as a beautiful white limestone temple 3000 years ago.

With the coming of Islam, mosques were built on most islands and on **Vaadhoo** it is said that the resident mosque was built by the actual founder of the Islamic culture in Maldives, Abu al-Barakat Yusuf al-Barbari.

The finely woven sleeping and praying mats that adorn houses nationwide are made by the women of **Gadhdhoo** and are called *thundu kunaa*.

Below: *The end of another perfect day in paradise!*

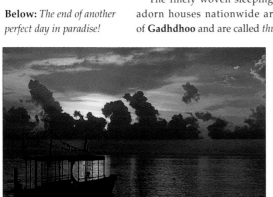

Thinadhoo, which is the capital of Gaafu Dhaalu, was once the stronghold of the secessionist movement. In 1962 the island was attacked by the superior Malé forces and the islanders were then banished to another island – the rapid end of a rather short-lived movement!

Gnaviyani (Foammulah) Atoll

This atoll is divided from Huvadhoo Atoll (Gaafu Alifu and Gaafu Dhaalu) by the **Equatorial Channel** which is 43km (25 miles) wide. A small atoll, Gnaviyani is one of the most isolated islands of the archipelago.

The lagoon and channel into the atoll have silted up with time and filled in to form one large island, 6km (4 miles) by 3km (2 miles), with two freshwater lakes. The protecting atoll reef that once surrounded the lagoon has become the island's fringing reef. Safe mooring for visiting ships is only found in the open sea on the lee side of the prevailing monsoon but a new harbour has been built. Even in its isolation the island is quite self-sufficient.

Inhabited for thousands of years, the island has had some well-known visitors. Ibn Battutah rested on the island in 1344 while waiting for the monsoon that would take him across to the Malabar coast. H.C.P. Bell, the archaeologist who spent a lot of time digging on the islands of the archipelago, visited Foammulah in 1922 to study its many ruins. Of the interesting sites to be explored on the island, the **Kedeyre Mosque** has a beautiful sunken ceremonial bath enclosed by well-fitted cut stone blocks that probably allowed water to filter through.

Seenu (Addu) Atoll

Seenu is about 480km (298 miles) from the capital of Malé and is the southernmost section of Maldives. But this atoll is not just a forgotten, tropical paradise, floating on tepid ocean waters. The islands of Seenu Atoll have played an important part in the economic and political development of the southern atolls. The capital, **Hithadhoo**, is the second-largest city in Maldives and has a regional hos-pital, schools, a vocation centre and an Islamic Centre. The British, who inhabited the island of **Gan** and developed the airforce base, also linked the string of islands that stretch along the atoll's southwestern boundary with the longest road in the country, which joins the islands of **Feydhoo**, **Maradhoo** and **Hithadhoo.**

The Maldives

Kaashidhoo Kandu

Malé
Vaadhoo Kandu

Felidhu Kandu

Vattaru Kandu

Kudahuvadhoo Kandu

Veimandu Kandu

One-and-a-half Degree Channel (Huvadhoo Kandu)

Equator   Equatorial Channel (Addoo Kandu)

ATOLL FACTS AND FIGURES

**Gaafu Alifu
(North Huvadhoo)**
Total population 8323; about 83 uninhabited islands; 10 inhabited islands; no resorts; capital Viligili.
**Gaafu Dhaalu
(South Huvadhoo)**
Total population 12,000; about 154 uninhabited islands; 10 inhabited islands; no resorts; capital Thinadhoo.
Gnaviyani (Foammulah)
Total population 7243; no uninhabited islands; one inhabited island; no resorts; capital Foammulah.
Seenu (Addu)
Population 18,000; 30 uninhabited islands, 7 inhabited; one resort; capital Hithadhoo.

RESORT ISLAND (EQUATOR VILLAGE)

Today the southernmost atoll sees few foreign visitors in comparison to the more popular Central Atolls and their resort islands. This is probably due to the fact that this atoll has been rather spoilt by the British who built an airstrip there. This has had a huge effect on the quality of the water and natural sand movement. So this area is largely for those who want to experience Maldives and their people rather than the beaches and the reefs.

Equator Village **

The resort island called Equator Village is on **Gan** Island in the Seenu (Addu) Atoll and is 380km (236 miles) south of Hulhule. Seenu is the last atoll of the Maldivian archipelago. You would definitely need to fly and flying time is about 90 minutes. The island is 2.4km (1½ miles) long which is large in comparison to some islands in Maldives.

The old officers' quarters have been converted into 78 rooms with air conditioning, hot and cold water, fridge and telephone. Facilities include a restaurant, bars, gym, pool, disco and shop. Sports available on the island are tennis, volleyball, badminton, table tennis, and water sports including scuba diving and catamaran sailing, which are standard for most of the resorts. Excursions are island-hopping, aerial photoflips and fishing.

Right: *Men, home from the resort islands where they work, enjoy the company of their children in the shade of a village tree.*

Central and Southern Atolls at a Glance

BEST TIMES TO VISIT

The dry monsoon (known as *iruvai* by Maldivians) between the months of **November** and **April** brings the clear, blue skies and the calmest seas. This is the best time for holiday-makers. During the rest of the year there are often storms and tropical rain showers. There is not much difference in terms of sunshine between the Maldivian seasons, but a substantial difference in the amount of rainfall they experience.

GETTING THERE

Charter flights and national airlines from many international destinations have regular flights that land at Hulhule, Maldives International Airport. From there the resort islands organise their own airport to island transfers either by private speed boat or sea plane. Visitors to the Equator Village on Addu Atoll take an Island Aviation flight which offers an excellent opportunity to photograph the atolls.

GETTING AROUND

It is almost impossible to travel between resorts in these remote atolls except on organised excursions booked at your resort. Tourists may only stay in accommodation provided by one of the seven resorts in these central and southern atolls. It is possible to visit the other islands within Addu Atoll after procuring relevant permission from the Ministry of Atolls Administration. The Southern Islands of Addu Atoll; Hithadhoo, Hankehdeh, Maradhoo, Feydhoo and Gan are connected by a bridging road built by the British. Tourists may hire bicycles or motorbikes to visit the islands.

WHERE TO STAY

Central Atolls
Meemu Atoll
Medhufushi Island Resort, tel: 46-0026, fax: 46-0027; Malé, tel: 31-6131, fax: 33-1726.
Hakuraa Club, tel: 46-0014, fax: 46-0013; Malé, tel: 31-3738, fax: 31-6264.

Faafu Atoll
Filitheyo Island Resort, tel: 46-0025, fax: 46-0024; Malé, tel: 31-6131, fax: 33-1726.

Dhaalu Atoll
Velavaru Island Resort, tel: 46-0028, fax: 46-0029; Malé, tel: 31-3914, fax: 31-5286.
Vilu Reef Beach and Spa Resort, tel: 46-0011, fax: 46-0022; Malé, tel: 32-5977, fax: 32-0419.

Southern Atolls
There is just one resort in the southern atolls, that being Addu Atoll:

Addu Atoll
Equator Village, tel: 58-8721, fax: 58-8020; Malé, tel: 32-2212, fax: 31-8057.

WHERE TO EAT

All the resorts have at least one restaurant and there is usually a coffee shop serving snacks. For resorts that have more than one restaurant it is advisable to book a half-board package instead of full-board.

TOURS AND EXCURSIONS

These are usually booked on a daily basis from the reception. It is advisable to make a reservation a day in advance. Diving, snorkelling and fishing is available on all these resort islands.

USEFUL CONTACTS

Addu Development Authority, Mannaarudhushuge, Henveiru, Malé, tel: 32-3101/6167.
Ministry of Atolls Administration, Faashanaa Building, Marine Drive, Malé, tel: 31-6512, 31-3816, 31-6776 or 32-3070, fax: 32-5499.
Maldives Tourism Promotion Board, Aage Building, 3rd Floor, 12 Boduthakurufaanu Magu, Malé 2004, tel: 32-3228, fax: 32-3229, website: www.visitmaldives.com e-mail: mtpb@ visitmaldives.com

4
Northern Atolls

Less crowded, the northern atolls stretch up to their sister archipelago, the beautiful **Lakshadweep** (formerly Laccadive) Islands, which were once part of the same group but somehow were separated on paper by an Arab cartographer, and later fell under the jurisdiction of India. However, the Maldivian fishermen of the northern islands see no boundaries. They fish in Lakshadweep waters and exchange greetings in Dhivehi with the locals who may have wandered south. In the lonely reality of this desolate world, imaginary geographical lines have no meaning; the immediate reality of life has far greater importance.

The weather pattern that sweeps past these northern reaches of Maldives is unpredictable and devastating. Hurricanes have been known to wash away entire islands, but reefs are separated by deep and wide channels making navigation an easier feat than in the southern reefs. Although there are several differences distinguishing the northern atolls from the rest of the archipelago, life on the fishing islands is practically unchanged.

THE NORTHERN ATOLLS
Lhaviyani (Faadhippolhu) Atoll

Situated north of Kaafu Atoll (North and South Malé Atoll), and separated by the **Kaashidhoo Channel**, is Lhaviyani Atoll. It is part of the Northern Atolls of Maldives and is about 120km (75 miles) from Hulhule International Airport. On the western rim, **Naifaru** is the capital island of the atoll with a population of over 3500.

Opposite: *Kuredu Island was the first resort to be developed in Lhaviyani Atoll and it now has 300 rooms on offer.*

Right: *Long and narrow, the island of Kuredu is surrounded almost in its entirety by a stunning beach.*

FACTS AND FIGURES

• **Lhaviyani (Faadhippolhu) Atoll:** population 9000; about 46 uninhabited islands, 5 inhabited islands and 5 resort islands; capital Naifaru.

• **Baa (South Maalhosmadulu) Atoll:** population 9000; about 63 uninhabited islands, 13 inhabited islands, 5 resorts; capital Eydhafushi.

• **Raa (North Maalhosmadulu) Atoll:** population 13,900; about 70 uninhabited islands, 15 inhabited islands, one resort, capital Ugoofaaru.

• **Noonu (South Miladhunmadulu) Atoll:** population 10,900; about 60 uninhabited islands, 14 inhabited islands, no resorts; capital Manadhoo.

• **Shaviyani (North Miladhunmadulu) Atoll:** 11,900; about 35 uninhabited islands, 15 inhabited islands, no resorts; capital Funadhoo.

• **Haa Dhaalu (South Thiladhunmathi) Atoll:** population 16,800; about 20 uninhabited islands, 16 inhabited islands, no resorts; capital Nolhivaranfaru.

• **Haa Alifu (North Thiladhunmathi) Atoll:** population 14,000; about 25 uninhabited islands, 16 inhabited islands, no resorts; capital Dhidhdhoo.

The nearby **Felivaru** has been the site of a fish canning factory since 1977; tonnes of tuna are processed and canned daily and exported worldwide. Freezer container ships were used to collect the processed fish from this island and, during a storm, one of these ships inadvertently crashed onto the reef and sunk to its watery grave. Today the site is known as 'The Shipyard' by the scuba diving community. Another ship was laid to rest on the same spot, the rusting carcass now part of the reef system of the atoll, covered in brightly coloured soft corals. There are five resort islands and 50 uninhabited islands in the atoll. On a few uninhabited islands such as **Dhiffushi** and **Huruvalhi**, the remains of mosques indicate that they too were once inhabited.

Kuredu Island Resort (Kuredhoo) ★★
Kuredu Island Resort is situated 148km (92 miles) north of Hulhule, on the northern rim of **Lhaviyani Atoll**. Transfer is approximately 40 minutes by seaplane, or four hours by fast speedboat.

The island is 1.6km (1 mile) long and narrow with beautiful beaches and a very large shallow lagoon on the south side. Accommodation is in 300 recently renovated cottages and water bungalows, all with hot water, air conditioning, phone and mini bar. Most are located on the edge of the beach close to the water. This is a beautiful island with an excellent dive school, good watersports facilities and a luxurious spa.

Komandoo Island Resort *

The only resort located on the west side of the atoll, Komandoo is a tiny island just 500m by 100m and surrounded by a beautiful beach. Accommodation is in 45 well-equipped individual cottages built in the shape of a shell and situated close to the water's edge.

One and Only Kanuhura ***

Located on the eastern rim of the atoll, Kanuhura is a long thin island 1000m by 200m with a shallow lagoon

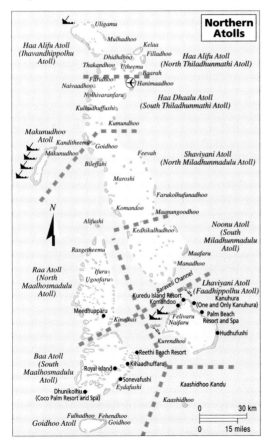

Northern Atolls

Uligamu
Mulhadhoo
Kelaa
Haa Alifu Atoll
(Ihavandhippolhu Atoll)
Dhidhdhoo
Filladhoo
Haa Alifu Atoll
Thakandhoo
Utheemu
(North Thiladhunmathi Atoll)
Faridhoo
Baarah
Naivaadhoo
Hanimaadhoo
Nolhivaranfaru
Haa Dhaalu Atoll
Kulhudhuffushi
(South Thiladhunmathi Atoll)
Kumundhoo
Makunudhoo
Atoll
Kanditheemu
Goidhoo
Makunudhoo
Feevah
Shaviyani Atoll
Bileffahi
(North Miladhunmadulu Atoll)
Maroshi
Farukolhufunadhoo
N
Komandoo
Maanungoodhoo
Alifushi
Noonu Atoll
Kedhikulhudhoo
(South
Rasgetheemu
Miladhunmadulu
Maafaru
Atoll)
Manadhoo
Raa Atoll
Ifuru
(North
Ugoofaru
Maalhosmadulu
Lhaviyani Atoll
Atoll)
Baraveli Channel
(Faadhippolhu Atoll)
Kuredu Island Resort
Kanuhura
Komandoo
(One and Only Kanuhura)
Meedhupparu
Felivaru
Palm Beach
Kinolhas
Naifaru
Resort and Spa
Hudhufushi
Kurendhoo
Baa Atoll
Reethi Beach Resort
(South
Kihaadhuffaru
Maalhosmadulu
Royal Island
Atoll)
Sonevafushi
Kaashidhoo Kandu
Dhunikolhu
Eydafushi
(Coco Palm Resort and Spa)
Kaashidhoo
Fulhadhoo Fehendhoo
Goidhoo Atoll
Goidhoo

0   30 km

0   15 miles

KUREDU PRO DIVERS

The diving school is an excellent five-star **PADI** diving facility. The school buildings include air-conditioned lecture rooms, a large equipment storage room with two freshwater basins for rinsing equipment and lots of hanging space, a well-stocked shop, video and camera hire, a workshop and a darkroom for processing film.
Pro Divers have a small army of diving instructors and a fleet of *dhonis* which they share with no other dive school, for diving expeditions to all corners of the atoll. With 48 dive sites to choose from, only one *dhoni* goes to a dive site at one time. Pro Divers offer a diversity of sites, from wrecks to tilas, channels and drift dives.

PRISONER IN MALDIVES

In 1602 the French explorer **François Pyrard** ran aground with his ship, *Corbin*, on the reef of the small atoll south of Baa Atoll. For five years he and his crew were held captive on **Fulhadhoo**. Here he wrote extensive accounts of their imprisonment. The captives' first chance of freedom came when a fleet from Bengal suddenly appeared on the horizon. The island king and the inhabitants fled at the sight of the fleet but François Pyrard and his castaway crew boarded the ships and were carried to freedom.

on the west side. The resort has excellent beaches and has been developed to provide a high standard of accommodation and facilities. There are 100 luxurious rooms, including water bungalows, suites, a spa, two restaurants, a mini-club and a freshwater pool. The sports facilities on the island are good.

Above: *Many resort islands are surrounded by a beautiful reef that is easily accessible from the beach.*

LACQUER WORK

The people of **Thulhaadhoo** are the skilful carvers of the small **lacquered boxes**, **plates** and **vases** that adorn the shop windows of Malé and the resort islands. Craftsmen sit informally in the shade of the island trees, carving from the local *funa* wood, better known as Alexandrian laurel. They then rub imported yellow, black and red resin sticks onto the wood and finish off their products with intricately carved floral patterns. The wooden ware is sought after not only by the tourists but by the islanders themselves who use the plates at religious and family festivals. The craft has brought great prosperity to the village.

Palm Beach Resort and Spa ***

Previously known as Madhiriguraidhoo, Palm Beach was opened in 1999 and provides accommodation in 100 air-conditioned rooms. This long thin island in the northeast corner of the atoll has stunning broad beaches, and the interior is densely vegetated with coconut palms. The resort has been developed to a high standard and offers the usual range of water sports.

Hudhufushi Island Resort

Located on the east side of the atoll in the centre of the very broad fringing reef, the island of Hudhufushi has been designated by the Government as a tourist island with 200 rooms, but the tender for its develoment has not yet been allocated. This is a beautiful V-shaped island with a shallow lagoon and mangroves growing in its centre. The surrounding beaches are stunning.

Baa (South Maalhosmadulu) Atoll

There is a small, lonely atoll called Goidhoo south of Baa Atoll that falls under the administrative jurisdiction of Baa Atoll. Because of its isolated location it has been a favourite for the banishing of outlaws and castaways. Since 1962 the three islands of the small atoll, **Fulhadhoo**, **Fehendhoo** and **Goidhoo**, have been used as open prisons.

Baa Atoll is about 145km (90 miles) from Malé and separated from Raa Atoll in the north by a narrow channel. The atoll distinguishes itself for its fine craftsmen and weavers. Lacquer work is done on the island of **Thulhaadhoo**; this craft has been revived since the advent of tourism which has created a demand for the beautiful, handcarved ornaments. The vases, lacquered in yellow, black and red resin, are intricately carved with flowery patterns. The capital island, **Eydhafushi**, was once famous for its weavers. However, since the importing of cheaper and easier-to-wash materials, the craft of weaving the heavy white cotton sarong, *feli*, is dying out. **Reethi Beach Resort**, just 600m by 200m has superb beaches and a stunning blue lagoon. Accommodation is in 100 thatched roof cottages designated as Standard, Deluxe or Water Villas. There are three restaurants, two bars and a coffee shop. Sports facilities include squash and tennis courts, the usual water sports, swimming pool and sauna. **Royal Island**, located in the centre of the atoll, is one of the most recent resorts to be developed. It has 152 bungalows and suites with air conditioning, hot and cold water; and a range of sports facilities. **Maldive Kihaad** is situated on the east side of Kihaadhuffaru Island. Accommodation comprises 100 bungalows, water bungalows and suites all with hot and cold water, some with air conditioning. The usual range of water sports is available. In the southwest of Baa Atoll, **Coco Palm Resort and Spa** has recently been developed on the island of Dhunikolhu to provide accommodation in 98 rooms. The island has beautiful broad beaches and a deep lagoon. Sports facilities are good.

Sonevafushi Resort ★★★

Sonevafushi Resort is 137km (85 miles) from the airport, located on the southern rim of the Baa Atoll. Seaplane transfer takes 35 minutes. One mile long (1.5km) and 600m (1969ft) wide, Sonevafushi is one of the larger resorts and offers its guests exclusivity and privacy. It is also one of the most expensive resorts in the Maldives. There are 65 rooms divided into superior rooms, duplex villas with an upstairs bedroom and a selection of Sonevafushi Villas. There is one restaurant that serves international cuisine, snack bar, spa and dive school.

BACK TO NATURE

Untouched, unspoilt and virtually unexplored, **Baa Atoll** offers great holiday opportunities for those seeking the natural Maldives, away from the hub of the Central Atolls. Soneva Fushi, which opened at the end of 1995, is the first tourist development of the atoll. **Turtles** nest on the island, and all precautions have been taken to ensure that they will return again and again as they have done for centuries before the intrusion of man. For the diving enthusiast, Baa Atoll has the reputation of having some of the best dive sites in Maldives.

Below: *Sonevafushi is one of the larger resort islands of the Maldives. It is blessed with beautiful beaches and a spectacular house reef.*

Below: *A Maldivian traditional dancer is caught up in the frenzy of the music.*

Raa (North Maalhosmadulu) Atoll

This atoll is separated from the Baa Atoll by a small 2km (1.2 mile) channel. Locally, it is famous for its boat builders and carpenters.

Through the years it has been visited by celebrated guests and VIP's from Malé. According to one of the legends, it is about 2000 years ago that Koimala Kaloa arrived on the beautiful island of **Rasgetheemu** with his royal Sri Lankan wife. They decided to settle here and were crowned king and queen by the locals.

Ibn Battutah, the famous 14th-century Arab traveller, landed on one of the southern islands during his first visit to Maldives. During his stay, the islanders' warmth and hospitality convinced him to prolong his sojourn on the archipelago for over a year.

The isolated northern island of **Alifushi** is the site of a modern boatyard where naval architects have studied and modified the traditional design of the local fishing *dhonis* to incorporate the more efficient use of diesel power. The boatyard produces several dozen large *dhonis* every year.

Meedhupparu Island Resort

The first and, to date, only resort in Raa Atoll is situated in the centre of the atoll 130km (80 miles) from Malé. This large resort has 215 rooms of two standards; bungalows and suites with air conditioning, hot and cold water. The resort has good beaches and diving facilities, but is a long way from the atoll perimeter and accessible channel diving. There is a tennis court and swimming pool on the island.

Noonu (South Miladhunmadulu) Atoll

Stretching northwards, above Raa Atoll, the last reaches of the Maldivian islands line up along a single long atoll and end with the smaller **Ihavandhippolhu Atoll**. For administrative purposes these two atolls have been grouped together and the larger atoll divided into four smaller groups: **Noonu** (South Miladhunmadulu), **Shaviyani** (North Miladhunmadulu), **Haa Dhaalu** (South Thiladhunmathi) and **Haa Alifu** (North Thiladhunmathi).

Shaviyani (North Miladhunmadulu) Atoll

The administrative capital island of the atoll is **Farukolhufunadhoo**, more commonly known as **Funadhoo**. The original inhabitants settled on this island because of its excellent harbour. Some of the other islands of Shaviyani stand out for their unique features like **Maanungoodhoo**, which has its own freshwater lake and is expanding yearly with

the rising water table. On the island of **Kandithmeemu**, the oldest known written sample of Thaama script was found. It is inscribed in the door frame of the main mosque and dates back to AD1588.

Above: *Here, men beat the Bodu Beru drums at a resort island.*

Haa Dhaalu (South Thiladhunmathi)

The island of **Hanimaadhoo** has Maldives' northernmost airstrip. This atoll boasts one of the country's most populated islands. **Kulhudhuffushi** supports a population of 5000, it has a regional hospital, a modern harbour and a wide waterfront where the inhabitants meet after sundown. The entrance channel to the harbour is dredged regularly, keeping it clear of sand build-up.

Most men now work aboard large ships and on faraway tourist islands to enrich their families' income. Those that have stayed behind have gained the reputation of being some of the best shark fishermen in the country.

Unique to this atoll is **Faridhoo**, the highest island of the republic, all of 3m (10ft) above sea level! Faridhoo is found in the central northern section on the border with Haa Alifu Atoll. Ruins of *hawittas* are found on several islands, but very little remains of the plundered ancient temples, as the locals used the cut stone in order to build their homes.

> ### SHIPWRECKS
>
> **Makunudhoo** is the only inhabited island of the elongated, small atoll found southwest of **Haa Dhaalu Atoll**. The 25km long (16 mile) reef system has been a major hazard to shipping since sea travellers ventured into the Indian Ocean. Taken by surprise by the sudden storms that erupt in the area, ships have been wrecked on this treacherous reef making the area a salvage diver's delight. The *Persian Merchant* is the oldest wreck (it sank in 1658). The *Heyston*, the *Royal Family* and the *George Reid* are three English ships that went down in the 1800s.

THE LAST OUTPOST

United administratively to Haa Alifu but separated by a 5km wide (3 mile) channel, **Ihavandhippolhu** is the northernmost atoll of the Maldivian Republic. It is also at the mercy of the open Indian Ocean swells that pound its outer reefs. The girls of the island of **Huvarafushi** are well known throughout the archipelago for their music and their dancing which they perform regularly. Inhabited since early times, the island has a mosque dated 1692, and in keeping with the pace of modernity, a fish freezing plant was founded in 1981.

Below: *The sun sets in a perfect picture of peacefulness!*

Haa Alifu (North Thiladhunmathi) Atoll

This atoll is situated in the northern tip of the country, about 780km (174 miles) from the capital city of Malé, in Kaafu Atoll. There are no resorts on this atoll.

The beautiful island of **Utheemu** lies within the boundaries of the surrounding atoll reef which protects it from the pounding southwesterly surf, and it can only be reached by small boats. This is probably the most special island to the Maldivian people as it is the birthplace of the country's beloved and celebrated hero, **Mohammed Thakurufanu**. The sultan, together with his two brothers, defeated the Portuguese tyrants in 1573 and gained the independence of the Maldive islands.

Their house, a renovated wooden palace, has become a national shrine, drawing people from all over the archipelago. Even the president and his ministers make the pilgrimage on **Independence Day** to pay homage to their hero. The palace is a fine show of noble life. The small rooms are decorated with finely woven cotton hangings while the floor is covered with the finest coral sand. Traditionally crafted lacquer ware, elegant beds and ornamental wooden chests make up the sparse furnishings. A new structure added to the facilities offered on the island is the **Bodu Thakurufanu Memorial Centre** with a library and conference rooms.

The fishing village of **Thakandhoo** has the sad reminder of the ruthlessness of the Portuguese rulers (*see* p. 15). It is the burial site of one of the Utheemu brothers, who was caught during the struggle and beheaded by the cruel invaders.

At the tip of the long atoll, **Kelaa** is the site of a former British airbase built in 1934 and used during World War Two as a RAF seaplane lookout in the northern part of the Indian Ocean. Today Kelaa is a fertile and productive farming island.

Northern Atolls at a Glance

The northernmost part of the northern atolls is occasionally affected by tropical cyclones during the wet months between **May** and **October**. The two southernmost atolls of this section, the **Lhavinyani** and **Baa atolls**, are rarely affected by the temperamental weather patterns of the far north. As with the Central Atolls, the best time to visit is during the dry months between November and April when blue skies and calm seas are virtually guaranteed. During the remainder of the year the days might be cooled by storms and prolonged tropical showers.

Charter flights and national airlines from many international destinations have regular flights that land at Hulhule, Maldives international airport. From there the resort islands organise their own airport to island transfers either by speedboat or seaplane. Transfer to these northern atolls is usually by seaplane which takes 35–45 minutes flying time. Air transfers can only be made during daylight hours and tourists arriving on late night flights are sometimes required to stay in a hotel in Malé until a transfer can be arranged. Although there is an airstrip in Haa Dhaalu

Atoll, there are no resorts or accommodation for tourists in this atoll.
For the serious scuba diver, safari boats cruise these northern atolls.

Dhonis from resort islands take tourists to visit the various nearby local islands. The islands are so small and life so relaxed that transport is not required once on your resort island.

Lhaviyani Atoll
Kuredu Island Resort, tel: 23-0337, fax: 23-0332; Malé office tel: 32-6545, fax: 32-6544.
Komandhoo Island Resort, tel: 23-1010, fax: 23-1011; Malé office: Champa Trade and Travel, Champa Building, Malé office tel: 32-6545, fax: 32-6544.
One and Only Kanuhura, tel:23-0044, fax: 23-0033; Malé office tel: 31-3739, fax: 33-1781.
Palm Beach Resort and Spa, tel: 23-0084, fax: 23-0091; Malé office tel: 33-1997, fax: 33-2001.
Hudhufushi Island Resort, tel/fax number to be allocated when resort is developed.

Baa Atoll
Sonevafushi Resort, tel: 23-0304, fax: 23-0374; Malé office tel: 32-6685, fax: 32-0374.

Reethi Beach Island Resort, tel: 23-2626, fax: 23-2727; Malé office tel: 31-2626, fax: 31-2727.
Royal Island, tel: 23-0088, fax: 23-0099; Malé office tel: 31-6161, fax: 31-4565.
Kihaadhuffaru, tel: 23-6688, fax: 23-6633; Malé office tel: 32-3441, fax: 32-2964.
Coco Palm Resort, tel: 23-0011, fax: 23-0022; Malé office tel: 32-4658, fax: 32-5543.

This is a selection of over 80 registered safari boats in the country:
Adventurer, tel: 32-6734, www.maldivesdiving.com
Keema, tel: 31-3539, www.interlinkmaldives.com
Island Explorer, tel: 44-4888, www.fourseasons.com
Sting Ray, tel: 31-4841, www.maldivesboatclub.com.mv
Horizon, tel: 32-1169, www.blue-horizon.com.mv
All the resort islands offer daily excursions island hopping, day or night fishing, snorkelling and aerial photoflips.

Maldives Tourism Promotion Board, Aage Building, 3rd Floor, 12 Boduthakurufaanu Magu, Malé 2004, tel: 32-3228, fax: 32-3229, www.visitmaldives.com e-mail: mtpb@visitmaldives.com

5
North Malé Atoll

Situated in the northern section and forming part of the central chain of Maldivian atolls, **North Malé Atoll** is the largest of the four that comprise the administrative **Kaafu Atoll** (*see* p. 39).

The northernmost of Kaafu's four atolls is actually a large island called **Kaashidhoo**, in the centre of the **Kaashidhoo Channel** that separates North Malé from Lhaviyani Atoll.

Close to the northern rim of North Malé is a small, oval-shaped atoll while to the south, separated by the narrow **Vaadhoo Channel,** is **South Malé Atoll**.

North Malé is the hub of Maldives. With the republic's capital city, **Malé**, situated on its southern rim, its waters are the country's equivalent of a spaghetti junction of highways. Surrounding Malé, the quiet waters inside the atoll offer protection to visiting and trading ships. *Dhonis* carry cargo from the ships to the capital as the inner harbour is too shallow for these shipping giants. Taxi *dhonis* ferry tourists and businessmen between the airport and the capital while an ever-increasing number of speedboats churn up the waters as they hurry to their resort island destinations. And through the tidal wake of modernity, fishing *dhonis*, unchanged in their design for centuries, routinely bring their catch to the fish market.

Traditional fishing islands enjoy the spoils of being surrounded by tourist resorts – making a profitable income from visiting tourists who buy their souvenirs. **Himmafushi** and **Huraa** are two such villages.

The Maldives

Kaashidhoo Kandu

Malé
Vaadhoo Kandu

Felidhu Kandu

Vattaru Kandu

Kudahuvadhoo Kandu

Veimandu Kandu

One-and-a-half Degree Channel (Huvadhoo Kandu)

Equator

Equatorial Channel (Addoo Kandu)

Opposite: *Strangely-shaped thatched roofs are characteristic of Thulhaagiri Island Resort.*

UTILIZED ISLANDS

Maafushi (South Malé Atoll) is the home of orphans and young delinquents. A children's reformatory was opened here in 1979 and is geared towards the rehabilitation and training of the wayward youngsters. **Dhoonidhoo** (North Malé Atoll) was the residence of the former British governor. Now, however, the modest bungalow is often used to house political prisoners. **Funadhoo** (North Malé Atoll) is the temporary home of government workers who maintain the oil tanks.

FERIA SUB AQUA

Feria Sub Aqua on **Bandos** is a large and efficient diving school. The diving centre was rebuilt and enlarged in 1995 to accommodate the ever-increasing number of scuba divers who frequent the resort. During peak season the centre can easily cope with over 100 divers a day. The school has three large fibreglass *dhonis* fast enough to reach the furthest dive sites on day excursions. Spacious and comfortable, the *dhonis* take up to 20 divers to dive sites such as **Maldives Victory**, **Barracuda Giri**, **Lion's Head** and **Banana Reef**. Dives on the house reef may be done throughout the day and night (provided you have a dive buddy, of course). Feria Sub Aqua has dive bases on several other resort islands.

RESORT ISLANDS

Due to their proximity to the capital and the airport, the uninhabited islands of North Malé Atoll were the first to accommodate and welcome tourists. The huts that were built in 1972 were simple, thatched bungalows that were later developed into stylish holiday resorts. There are 27 resort islands in **North Malé Atoll**, including **Kurumba**, which was the first resort to be built in Maldives.

All the islands are similar: coconut palms and green bush, sugar-white sand and crystal-clear lagoons. Making a choice is difficult and depends more on whether you want the very best there is to offer with all the modern conveniences, or simple, rustic accommodation without television or a telephone.

Asdu Sun Island *

This small resort is situated 37km (23 miles) northeast of Hulhule International Airport. The transfer takes either three hours by *dhoni*, 30 minutes by speedboat or 15 minutes by seaplane.

Asdu Sun Island offers 30 standard bungalows for guests and there is a restaurant, bar and little shop selling necessities and postcards. Table tennis and volleyball are recreations offered on the island and water-sports enthusiasts can scuba dive, snorkel, windsurf, water-ski and canoe. Excursions are island-hopping, aerial photoflips and fishing.

Bandos **

Built in 1972, Bandos was the second Maldivian resort to be dedicated to the tourist. Situated 8km (5 miles) north of the airport in North Malé Atoll the transfer to Bandos Resort Island takes 45 minutes by *dhoni* or 15 minutes by speedboat. The spacious island offers a multitude of settings: spacious palm-fringed beaches alternate with secluded private beaches – all a few swimming strokes away from the surrounding house reef which is a snorkelling paradise. Pathways, like the streets of a village, are infused with the scent of frangipani.

North Malé Atoll

Gaafaru Falhu
Gaafaru
Gaafaru Kandu

North Malé Atoll (Kaafu Atoll)

Akirifushi
Helengeli

N

Eriyadhoo

Makunudhoo
Summer Island
One and Only
Reethi Rah
(Opening Dec 2004)
Hembadhoo
(Taj Coral Reef)
Asdu Sun Island
Meeru Island Resort

Boduhithi (Coral Island)
Kudahithi (Relais)
Dhiffushi

Huvafen Fushi
Gasfinolhu (Mahureva)
Thulusdhoo
Kanifinolhu (Club Med)
Lhohifushi
Vabbinfaru
Huraa
(Banyan Tree)
Thulhaagiri
Himmafushi
Kuda Huraa (Four Seasons)
Ihuru (Angsana
Resort and Spa)
Kanuhuraa (Dhonveli Beach)
Baros
Lankanfushi (Soneva Gili)
Bandos
Lankanfinolhu
(Paradise)
Furanafushi
(Full Moon)
Kurumba
Farukolhufushi
Village
(Club Med)
Giraavaru

Hulhule
0   10 km

Viligili
Vaadhoo Kandu
Malé
0   5 miles

Above: *Reversing onto Bandos Beach, this majestic seaplane offloads and collects its passengers.*
Opposite: *Summer Island on the northwestern side of North Malé Atoll is one of the cheapest and simplest tourist island resorts.*

ISLAND TRANSFERS

Dhonis are slow, motorized local boats. They provide a leisurely ride when the sea is calm and the weather is good. **Speedboats** vary in size from large passenger carriers to smaller ones used by the islands. The most romantic way to get to an island, though, is by **seaplane**. The mode of transport for tourists is usually pre-arranged when booking a tour package. Transfers to the more remote islands cannot be made at night so visitors arriving on these flights may have to stop over in Malé prior to transfer.

WHY NOT FLY!

The option of flying to resorts that are a fair distance from the airport may not be included in your holiday package, but, for an added fee, you can easily fly by seaplane to most island resorts (provided that they are not too close to the airport). Not only is it considerably quicker, but you will also have the opportunity of seeing the atolls, the reefs and the islands from the air. For those who have never been on a boat or who suffer from sea sickness, flying is definitely the better option!

Below: *The water villas at Baros are organized in a semicircle and extend their 'feet' into the calm waters of the lagoon.*

Bandos is a large, round island – it could almost be called a 'mini holiday city'. It has 225 luxury rooms and executive suites, lining the beachfront of the island. Each room has air conditioning, hot and cold water, a mini bar, telephone and hairdryer. There are several restaurants to choose from, including a chargrill restaurant, an Italian restaurant and a seafood restaurant.

The resort boasts a 24-hour coffee shop, several bars, a shopping arcade with a photographic shop, souvenir shops, a jewellery shop and business centre (with fax machines, a typist, computers, photostat machine – everything that an office should have) for the businessman who cannot stay away from the office. The modern convention centre has a conference room for 500 people.

The gymnasium includes a freshwater pool, spa bath, beauty salon, a children's room and playground with full-time babysitters. The fully-equipped medical centre has a doctor on call 24 hours a day and a four-man, DAN-approved hyperbaric chamber (the only one in the Maldives). Island sports that you can enjoy are tennis, badminton, soccer, aerobics and squash. Water sports available are scuba diving, snorkelling, windsurfing, catamaran sailing, canoeing, water-skiing, parasailing, banana boat and tube rides.

Excursions are arranged to Malé for shopping, as well as island-hopping, aerial photoflips and fishing. Two ferries a day take people to and from the uninhabited island of **Kuda Bandos** and once a week the management organizes an evening barbecue and live entertainment on the island.

Baros **

Baros is in the northwest of North Malé Atoll and the trip from the airport, a distance of 15km (10 miles) takes one hour by *dhoni* or, alternatively, 20 minutes by speedboat. From the air, Baros is shaped like a half-moon with a straight, expansive beach facing a deep blue lagoon.

The island is small – only 460m (1509ft) at its widest point. It has 59 bungalows tucked away in the island vegetation. Sixteen tastefully designed, Maldivian water villas lie in a semicircle within the lagoon's protective womb. Inside, wooden finishings and flowing, voile curtaining are the ideal setting for a peaceful rest as the gently lapping water lulls you to sleep. All have air conditioning, hot and cold water, a mini bar and a hairdryer. Facilities on the island include a sand-floor restaurant, an open-air coffee shop with a separate barbecue terrace, bar, disco and a souvenir shop. Beach volleyball, scuba diving, catamaran sailing, windsurfing and water-skiing are offered. A rich reef surrounds the island which is perfect for snorkelling. Baros organizes Malé shopping excursions, island-hopping and fishing trips.

Boduhithi Coral Island ★★★

Situated on the western rim of North Malé Atoll, 24km (15 miles) from Hulhule, transfer to the island is about one hour by speedboat.

This large and lively Italian resort has 82 bungalows and 21 water villas, all with air conditioning, fridge, telephone, and private safe deposit box. The resort has two restaurants, a souvenir shop, bar, disco, small theatre, gymnasium and medical centre.

Beach volleyball, table tennis and soccer are played on the island. Excursions and water sports are standard as offered in most resorts (snorkelling and scuba diving being the main attraction in Maldives). The island is situated on the Boduhithi Channel where, seasonally, grey reef sharks and eagle rays gather in the current, offering stunning opportunities for the underwater photographer.

> **MALÉ SHOPPING**
>
> The resorts that are close to the capital city offer (at an extra charge) a day excursion to Malé. A guide will take you for a walk through the city, past all the best sights and then to the shopping street. Don't stop and buy in the first shop you enter. Rather look around for the best price and bargain with the shop owners. Those islands that are too far away from the capital usually organize that you reach the airport well before your return flight is due to leave. This allows you enough time to catch a taxi *dhoni* to Malé for some last-minute sightseeing and shopping.

Below: *The calm waters of the lagoons offer the perfect setting for windsurfing.*

EXCURSIONS

These are offered on most of the resort islands in Maldives. Half-day excursions are organized in the morning and afternoon. These trips include *dhoni* trips to other islands, snorkelling trips (**safaris**) to submerged reefs or uninhabited islands and visits to **fishing villages**. The excursions are optional extras and you usually have to pay a surcharge. If your resort island does not have a house reef or if it is too far away for guests to swim to, snorkelling trips are usually arranged free of charge. Full-day excursions include trips to other atolls and island-hopping during which you may visit other resort islands, fishing villages and have a barbecue lunch on a deserted island.

Club Med Faru (Farukolhufushi) ★★★

The grand resort island of Club Med is 6ha (15 acres) in size and closest to the airport. It is situated on the eastern rim of the atoll, directly north of the runway so it takes only 30 minutes by *dhoni* to get there. It is popular with young, fun-loving people. Children are not allowed.

Most of the main buildings were rebuilt in 1994 after a fire destroyed the shapely roofs that distinguished the resort from all of the others. Included in the holiday package are all water sports and one dive a day for qualified divers.

Guests are accommodated in 152 bungalows set in two-storey buildings, all with air conditioning but only cold water showers. One restaurant offers buffet-style meals, another specializes in Oriental cuisine. There is a bar, gymnasium, swimming pool, arts and crafts workshop, table tennis tables, disco, conference facilities as well as wild entertainment every night. Mini-football, aerobics, volleyball and petanque, scuba diving, snorkelling, catamaran sailing, windsurfing and canoeing are the activities available and the standard resort excursions are offered.

Eriyadhoo ★★

The resort island is 42km (26 miles) from Hulhule International Airport, near the northern tip of North Malé Atoll. The transfer is usually by speedboat and takes one hour.

This small island has 57 palm-thatched bungalows surrounded by a large beach and plenty of trees. Facilities include a restaurant, a shop selling souvenirs, and a bar. Excursions are standard. Being alone in the far north of the atoll, Eriyadhoo shares dive sites with an occasional dive boat from another resort. A wide beach lines the water's edge and a beautiful house reef encircles the island. In fact, the resort boasts of having the best house reef in the North Malé Atoll!

Full Moon Beach Resort (Furana) ★★★

Full Moon 3km (2 miles) from the airport is a large, luxury resort, on the eastern rim of the atoll.

It has 104 luxury rooms set in two-storey guesthouses and 52 water bungalows, all with air conditioning, hot and cold water, a mini bar, telephone and hairdryer.

Three restaurants – a Thai and Mediterranean restaurant and a barbecue terrace – provide excellent food for hungry guests. There is also an international coffee shop. The bar is stunning – it has a wooden terrace over the lagoon, and there is also a piano bar, disco, and a large fresh-water swimming pool. Full Moon has a gymnasium with a jacuzzi and a business centre available for the convenience of the discerning guest.

Sports and excursions are standard but Full Moon is a top-of-the-range resort with five-star luxury only a few minutes away from the airport. White beaches and calm lagoons are complimented by a house reef within easy reach of snorkellers.

Mahureva (Gasfinolhu) ★★★

Mahureva, an extremely small, high-range resort on the eastern rim of North Malé Atoll is 18km (11 miles) north of the airport. Transfer takes 90 minutes by *dhoni* or 30 minutes by speedboat. The original Dhivehi name of the island, Gasfinolhu, which means 'tree on a sand bank', gives an idea of the size of this exclusive resort. It only has 40 luxury bungalows and a restaurant, bar and shop.

Sports on the island are table tennis and beach volleyball. Water sports are standard resort recreations. Half- and full-day excursions, Malé shopping trips, aerial photoflips and fishing are on offer to an exclusive Italian clientele.

Above: *Full Moon's 52 water villas, overlooking the house reef, offer opulent luxury.*
Opposite: *For those who do not like to get their towels and bathing suits full of sand, beach chairs are supplied.*

THE GIRAAVARU PEOPLE

The resort island of Giraavaru was once the home of the aboriginal inhabitants of Maldives. They were moved to the capital city after erosion affected their island. Throughout the centuries they have kept to themselves and have tried to maintain their identity. They believe that their ancestors are the **Tamil** from **south India** and they follow different customs and speak with a different accent. Today their numbers are slowly dwindling as the young are becoming assimilated into Maldivian society.

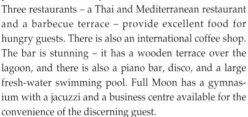

Above: *Beach volleyball is a popular sport on resort islands.*
Opposite: *The Maldives is a wonderful place for youngsters to learn to swim and snorkel.*

CORAL-MINING

With the introduction of tourism, massive population growth and the increased wealth of the Maldives, demand for building material has grown substantially. Until recently, large *Porites* corals were being taken from the house reefs of locally inhabited islands. The government is deeply concerned about the environmental implications of this and in 1992 introduced regulations to control coral-mining activities. Mining can no longer be carried out on island house reefs, on atoll rim reefs or bait-fishing reefs.

Giraavaru **

Giraavaru, a low-range resort along the southern rim on the **Vaadhoo Channel**, is situated 11km (7 miles) to the west of the airport. Transfer takes approximately 45 minutes by *dhoni* or 20 minutes by speedboat.

The 66 air-conditioned bungalows, each with a television, phone and fridge, have sea views. It has a restaurant, two bars, a coffee shop, curio shop, disco, freshwater swimming pool and spa. The water sports and excursions offered are the same as on most islands and you can also play tennis, beach volleyball and table tennis. Fine beaches, good snorkelling and famous shark diving sites are the main attractions of the island.

Helengeli *

This medium-range resort island is 51km (32 miles) north of Hulhule, on the far northeastern rim of North Malé Atoll. If you are transferred by speedboat it will take two hours but, if you travel by seaplane, it will take about 20 minutes. The island is 800m (2625ft) long and 150m (492ft) wide. There are 50 modern sea-facing bungalows with air conditioning and hot water. A restaurant and bar provides distraction but there is no windsurfing, sailing or other water sports. Being so far north, Helengeli is the most isolated resort island of the atoll, but it is surrounded by an unspoiled house reef and very good dive sites. It is ideal for the visitor who wants a quiet holiday with a spectacular underwater experience.

Taj Coral Reef (Hembadhoo) **

Situated on the western rim of the atoll, the resort is 35km (22 miles) from the airport, 40 minutes by speedboat or 20 minutes by seaplane. This small island offers a high standard of accommodation (35 lagoon villas and 30 garden villas) and a range of facilities. All rooms have air conditioning and hot and cold water. There are two restaurants and a terrace bar. Sports facilities include a fitness centre, swimming pool, catamarans, windsurfers and canoes.

Soneva Gili Resort (Lankanfushi) ★★★

This high-range resort, opened in 2001, is situated 10km (6 miles) north of Hulhule International Airport on the eastern rim of the atoll. It takes 50 minutes by *dhoni* to reach it.

This small island has 44 beautifully appointed timber and glass villas, 7 of which float in the lagoon and are accessed by private boats. Buffet or à la carte meals are served in the restaurant. Facilities include a swimming pool, luxurious spa, dive and water-sports centre and free bicycles to get around the island. Excursions to Malé or local fishing villages can be arranged through reception. This is the perfect choice for relaxation in elegant surroundings.

Angsana Resort and Spa (Ihuru) ★★★

Small and round with a diameter of 150m (492ft), it takes only 15 minutes to walk around Ihuru which is also not far from the airport – only 17km (10 miles). The trip takes under an hour by *dhoni* or 20 minutes by speedboat.

The 45 beachfront villas have been recently renovated in contemporary style. They all have air conditioning, hot and cold water, a fridge, safe, separate dressing area and veranda with a Maldivian swing. There is a bar that stretches over the water, a shop, disco and spa. Beach volleyball, table tennis and badminton are resort recreations and water sports consist of scuba diving, snorkelling, windsurfing, catamaran sailing, parasailing, water-skiing, banana boat riding, canoeing and glass-bottom boat rental.

Ihuru offers all the standard excursions and is a typical island paradise. The main attraction of the island's waters is its **house reef** which may be classed as close to perfect. Five entry points have carefully been mapped out for scuba divers, offering a variety of dive sites.

By remaining environmentally friendly and by being actively involved in marine biology research, the resort has won two major environmental awards.

CHILD-FRIENDLY ISLANDS

Most resort islands welcome children, and the Maldivian staff (who are often separated from their own families) are invariably wonderful with children. Resorts that specifically cater for families and have children's play areas, crèches and/or activity programmes include Bandos Island Resort, Laguna Maldives, Lily Beach Resort, Four Seasons Island Resort and One and Only Kanuhura. Many, but not all, resorts provide cots, high chairs or a baby-sitting service. A few resorts have a 'no children' policy, so verify with your agent.

Keeping in the shade is difficult, so swimsuits with ultra-violet protection are great. Sunglasses, sunhats and sun block also help children play safely in the sun. Resort shops supply very few baby products, so best to bring all you need, especially nappies.

Club Med Kani (Kanifinolhu) **

Lying along the eastern rim of the atoll, its distance from the airport is 19km (12 miles) north. To reach this island it takes 90 minutes by *dhoni* or 30 minutes by speedboat. Kanifinolhu is large and beautiful with 145 palm-thatched bungalows. Each bungalow has air conditioning, hot and cold water, a mini bar and telephone.

The central, thatched complex includes a reception, well-stocked bar, restaurant and coffee shop. There is also a disco, curio shop and spa. Recreations on the island are standard and you can book excursions at reception.

EXOTIC ROOMS

Kudahithi has only seven bungalows on the island, each decorated in a style to suit all fantasies: there is the opulent **'Maharani's Room'**, the **'Rehendi's Room'** (Queen's Room), the **'Sheikh's Room'** with an enormous bath and the **'Captain's Cabin'**. The **'Safari Lodge'** is decorated in a distinct African style. The **'Maldivian Apartment'** has an outdoor bathroom set in a private garden, and the **'Balinese Room'** is also beautifully decorated.

Kudahithi Relais ***

It takes 30 minutes by speedboat to reach this high-range resort which is 26km (16 miles) northwest of the airport. Kudahithi is small, exclusive and was once a small spit of sand with two palm trees.

Guests are accommodated in seven exclusive bungalows each designed and decorated in exotic styles. All rooms have air conditioning, hot and cold water, TV, fridge, hairdryer, a large bathroom with a bath, a terrace and a telephone.

There is no evening entertainment on the island; the nearest nightlife can be found on the neighbouring island of Boduhithi. Kudahithi is geared for honeymooners and those who prefer the solitude of a small island. Water sports are snorkelling, windsurfing and canoeing and the island offers half- and full-day excursions.

Kurumba Village (Vihamanaafushi) ***

Closest to the airport, 3km (2 miles) to the north (30 minutes by *dhoni*), this was the first resort to be established in Maldives. Its accommodation has improved considerably since the first primitively built huts were scattered on the beach and it is now a high-range resort.

Kurumba is a cosmopolitan resort, well-suited for the sophisticated holiday-maker. It is also close enough to Malé for the businessman to escape to a pleasant environment away from the over-crowded capital city.

Kurumba reopened in early 2004 following major reconstruction. The 180 luxurious rooms are divided into seven catagories, some with private pool. There is a choice of seven restaurants: Kurumba Mahal (Indian), Ming Court (Chinese), Golden Cowrie (Western and Japanese), Vihamana (International buffets and table d'hôte), the new Al Qadir (Arabic), Barbecue Terrace (for under the stars dining) and the Pizza Piazza beside the swimming pool. There is also a 24 hour seaview coffee shop. Two bars, a disco and a nightclub take care of the entertainment. Other facilities include a gymnasium with a pool, a swimming pool, a games centre, a conference centre for 500 people, a banquet hall for 300 people, and shops. For sports enthusiasts the whole range of activities is available.

Being so close to the capital city, Malé shopping trips are a regular event, and excursions, aerial photoflips, fishing and rides in the glass-bottom boat can all be booked at reception.

Lhohifushi **

This is a medium-range resort, on the eastern rim, 18km (11 miles) northeast of the airport. Transfer from Hulhule takes 90 minutes by *dhoni* and 30 minutes if you arranged to travel by speedboat.

Guests are accommodated in 127 duplex-style bungalows with air conditioning and hot and cold water. There are three restaurants and a bar. A small gymnasium, a freshwater swimming pool and a disco are available for those guests who enjoy a lot of exercise. The resort is set on a beautiful lagoon perfect for windsurfing.

Above: *For those who prefer fresh water and sand-free sunbathing, Kurumba has a large, inviting pool.*
Opposite: *Canoeing is very popular among tourists as they can paddle over the shallow reef and admire the tremendous variety of fish.*

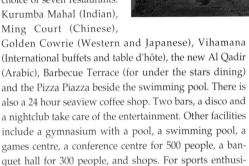

SURFING

It may come as a surprise that this holiday destination with some of the best scuba diving in the world also caters for surfers. On the outside of **North Malé Atoll** the **Indian Ocean** meets the reef and creates perfect waves! Surfing is possible all year round, but the best months are from May to October. North Malé resort islands for the surfer are: **Lhohifushi**, **Full Moon Beach Resort**, **Paradise Island** and **Dhonveli Beach**.

Four Seasons Resort (Kuda Huraa) ★★★

Recently redeveloped and now managed by the International Four Seasons group, this resort offers a high standard of accommodation and service. There are 106 bungalows and villas situated around the edge of the resort all with an ocean view. Rooms comprise 63 beach villas, 38 water villas and 5 pool beach villas. Water-sports facilities include canoeing and catamaran sailing and there is a swimming pool, sauna, spa and jacuzzi on the island. Business services include audiovisual equipment and 24-hour concierge services.

At low tide you can walk to nearby Huraa Island and Dhonveli Beach. These two islands were named after the Huraa Dynasty of sultans which was founded in 1759.

Above: *For the romantics, the seaplane is perfect for a ride above the islands that dot the Indian Ocean.*

A SEAPLANE PHOTOFLIP

If you do not fly to your resort island it will be worth your while to invest in a 15-minute seaplane excursion. The seaplanes can collect passengers from most of the islands either by boarding its passengers from a purpose-built floating jetty or by reversing onto the beach. A low 15-minute flight will allow you to photograph the island from the air as well as the atolls and reefs of the Maldives.

Makunudhoo Island ★★★

The distance from the airport is 34km (22 miles) and the island is situated in the northwest of the atoll. It takes almost three hours by *dhoni*, 55 minutes by speedboat or eight minutes by seaplane.

The size of this high-range resort is 2ha (6 acres). Guests are accommodated in 36 thatched bungalows with sitting area and outside Maldivian-style bathroom. Afternoon tea and cake is provided. The restaurant offers cuisine created by a European chef and there is a bar and snack shop. Fine amenities are available to guests at the resort.

Sports that are available include beach volleyball, badminton and table tennis while water sports on the island are scuba diving, snorkelling, windsurfing, catamaran sailing and water-skiing. Excursions include Malé shopping, half- and full-day excursions, a full moon picnic, and fishing. The beautiful island of Makunudhoo is richly covered in tropical vegetation and offers a quiet retreat for those seeking privacy and tranquillity.

Meeru Island Resort (Meerufenfushi) *

The easternmost resort island of Maldives and one of the country's largest, Meeru is 28ha (72 acres) in size. 'Meeru-fen-fushi' means 'sweet-water island' – the name given to it by the locals. It is 40km (25 miles) northeast of the airport. Travelling to Meeru takes about three hours by slow, motorized *dhoni* or over an hour by speedboat.

This popular, value-for-money resort has 227 Maldivian-style rooms ranging from standard, jacuzzi villas to honeymoon suites. All rooms have en-suite bathrooms, air conditioning, hot and cold water and sea views. Internet facilities and a spa are also available.

There is a huge open-air, semi-thatched, sand floor restaurant, 24-hour cocktail bar and a shop. The disco is open-plan with a sand floor. The coffee shop and outdoor bar overlook the huge lagoon. The resort has one of the largest swimming pools in the country and there is also a badminton hall.

Most visitors book at reception to go out on the morning snorkelling safaris as the best reefs are submerged and about 20 minutes from the island. A small fee is charged. You can also hire (at a price) one of the island's catamarans or windsurfers. There is an excellent diving school on Meeru and the underwater life is spectacular.

ISLAND SPORTS

Although Maldives is mainly about underwater and water sports, most islands offer some sort of landbased sport. **Volleyball** is the most popular, and is usually played on the beach at sundown. The islands large enough to have a **soccer field** build one in the centre of the island for their staff members. Holiday-makers are welcome and often encouraged to join in. **Table tennis** and **badminton** are popular and most islands offer both. The younger, up-market islands have a fully equipped **gymnasium** and a few have **tennis courts** and **fresh-water swimming pools**.

Huvafen Fushi Spa Resort ***

A brand new, top-class resort and first to boast an underwater spa and overwater yoga pavilion. There are 44 bungalows with plunge pools or jacuzzi pools and all have superb seaviews. One can relax at the infinity swimming pool or choose a book, CD or

Below: *Maldivian resorts offer the perfect setting for a romantic honeymoon.*

DELPHIS DIVING CENTRE

Patrons of the well-organized Delphis Diving Centre have only a few paces to go before boarding the *dhoni* for the daily scuba diving excursions on offer to any of the **40 mapped dive sites** within reach of **Paradise Island**. The sites include the famous local **Manta Point** where, between the months of May and November, mantas come in to feed and be cleaned. Tiled floors and paved walkways ensure that diving equipment does not get spoiled by the fine coral sand. Spacious, clean, well-equipped and efficient, this dive school makes diving a real pleasure.

DVD from the island library. For those feeling more energetic there is a dive school and water-sports centre. It is 24km (15 miles) northwest of the airport and the trip takes 90 minutes by mororized *dhoni* or 30 minutes by speedboat. Excursions such as sunset fishing, snorkelling and big-game fishing can all be arranged.

Paradise Island (Lankanfinolhu) ★★★

Land has been reclaimed on the southern end of the island to double its size. This is the resort with the most rooms in Maldives. There are 260 luxury rooms of which 40 are water villas built on stilts.

The dolphin-shaped swimming pool is very popular and there are four restaurants, a gymnasium with a steam bath and sauna, a conference room, shops, disco and entertainment rooms where there is something happening every night. Apart from the standard resort recreations, Paradise Island also has tennis, squash, badminton, basketball and aerobics. Excursions can be booked at the reception.

A few kilometres north of Full Moon (Furana Resort) is Paradise Island. This luxurious complex offers facilities and services of a high standard while not forgetting the 'island feel'. Neatly tiled pathways meander through the interior, past the sea-facing rooms and manicured gardens.

The resort's most outstanding features are two bars set over the water. The Sunrise Bar faces the open Indian Ocean. From it one can hear the crashing waves as they meet the fringing reefs of the atoll and see eagle rays and stingrays moving in the shallows.

The underwater drop-off offers a great house reef dive or snorkel. The enclosing wall that runs perpendicular to the long wooden jetty forms a small port with easy mooring for the island's speedboats and *dhonis*.

Below: *At the end of a long jetty, lined with luxurious water villas, the Sunrise Bar of Paradise Island almost reaches the outer wall of Malé's encircling reef.*

Left: *Striped dolphins* (Stenella coeruleoalba) *are among the most acrobatic and beautiful of all the dolphins found in the Maldives. They are fairly common in the offshore waters outside the atolls.*

One and Only Reethi Rah Resort

This resort is located 35km (22 miles) from Hulhule International Airport, on the western rim of the atoll.

The island is just 800m (2625ft) long and 100m (328ft) at its widest. Regular inhabitants of this part of the lagoon facing the open sea, are baby blacktip reef sharks looking for protection in the shallow waters, and small stingrays.

The protected waters surrounding the island are well suited for windsurfing, especially for beginners preferring the tranquillity of a lagoon. With such an expansive body of water the house reef is a fair way offshore.

The resort is currently closed for renovation and is due to re-open late 2004.

Dhonveli Beach (Kanuhuraa) ★★

Dhonveli Beach, on the eastern rim of the North Malé Atoll, is only 15km (10 miles) from the airport, so it takes 90 minutes by *dhoni* or 30 minutes by speedboat.

It's a small and intimate island, heavily covered in vegetation, and landscaped beach. Guests are accommodated in 50 cottages with air conditioning, hot and cold fresh water and a mini bar. The restaurant serves good food and you can spend time in the coffee shop or beach bar. Tennis, aerobics and beach volleyball are offered to the very energetic. The water sports and excursions are the same as for all the other resort islands. It is the country's most popular resort with surfers.

WHALE AND DOLPHIN WATCHING

Maldives is justly famous for its beach and diving holidays. It is now also gaining an international reputation for its whale and dolphin watching. Twenty one species have been recorded so far. The acrobatic spinner dolphin (*Stenella longirostris*) is the most common, and several resorts run afternoon boat trips to see them. But to appreciate the full diversity of species found locally book a dedicated whale and dolphin safari trip.

Thulhaagiri ★★★

Thulhaagiri is 11km (7 miles) from the airport and the trip takes one hour by motorized *dhoni* or 20 minutes by speedboat. The resort has developed a style of its own with exotically shaped thatched roofs over the pool bar and diving school. Soft sea sand covers all floors and pathways in typical Maldivian style. The 69 deluxe and spacious rooms include 17 water villas.

The resort has the usual amenities but it also has a pool and poolside bar. Water sports and excursions are standard. Small and quaint – it takes seven minutes to walk around the island – the atmosphere is kept alive by the constant chattering of the hundreds of budgies that have been left to fly around freely.

Banyan Tree (Vabbinfaru) ★★

A high-range resort 16km (10 miles) to the northwest. Transfer is one hour by *dhoni* or 20 minutes by speedboat. Lining the sandy beach are 48 luxurious thatch-roofed bungalows. This resort can easily be seen from the island of **Ihuru**. Facilities, excursions and resort recreations appeal to an international clientele.

Summer Island (Ziyaaraiyfushi) ★★

Fairly recently redeveloped, this all-inclusive resort is located 35km (22 miles) from Malé on the western rim of the atoll. Transfer to the island takes 90 minutes by fast *dhoni* and 20 minutes by seaplane.

Accommodation is in 108 simple air-conditioned bungalows built around the edge of the island, including 16 water villas with television. The resort is small – it takes 30 minutes to walk around it. The recreation facilities include a spa and weekly theme nights.

Below: *The Thulhaagiri budgie population started with a few specimens confined to a cage. Now the expanded colony of flyers are free to fly everywhere on the island.*

North Malé Atoll at a Glance

The resort islands are open all year round although the best time to visit is during the dry months between **November** and **April** when clear, blue skies are virtually an everyday occurrence. During the wet monsoon, between **May** and **October**, refreshing tropical showers relieve the heat.

Hulhule International Airport has connections to many European cities and many private yachts cruise the islands.

Taxi *dhonis* ferry people between Malé and Hulhule. Resort islands have their own boats to transport passengers – usually motorized dhonis or speedboats. Seaplanes fly between Hulhule and the other resort islands (see Travel Tips).

The islands all look similar but the style and standard of accommodation varies greatly.

North Malé Atoll
Angsana Resort and Spa, tel: 44-3502, fax: 44-5933; Malé, tel: 32-3369, fax: 32-4759.
Asdhu Sun Island, tel/fax: 44-5051; Malé, tel: 32-2149, fax: 32-4300.
Bandos, tel: 44-0088,

fax: 44-3877; Malé, tel: 32-1026, fax: 32-1026.
Banyan Tree, tel: 44-3147, fax: 44-3843; Malé, tel: 32-3369, fax: 32-4752.
Baros, tel: 44-2678, fax: 44-3497; Malé, tel: 32-3080, fax: 32-2678.
Boduhithi, tel: 44-3981, fax: 44-2634; Malé, tel: 31-3937, fax: 31-3939.
Club Med Kani, tel: 44-3152, fax: 44-4859.
Dhonveli Beach, tel: 44-0055, fax: 44-0012; Malé, tel: 32-2537, fax: 32-2798.
Eriyadhoo Island, tel: 44-4487, fax: 44-5926; Malé, tel: 31-6131, fax: 33-1726.
Farukolhufushi (Club Med Faru), tel: 44-3021, fax: 44-1997; Malé, tel: 32-2976, fax: 32-2850.
Four Seasons, tel: 44-4888, fax: 44-1188; Malé, tel: 32-5529, fax: 31-8992.
Full Moon (Furana), tel: 44-2010, fax: 44-1979; Malé, tel: 32-3080, fax: 32-2678.
Giraavaru, tel: 44-0440, fax: 44-4818; Malé, tel: 31-8422, fax: 31-8505.
Helengeli, tel: 44-4615, fax: 44-2881; Malé, tel: 32-8544, fax: 32-5150.
Huvafen Fushi, tel: 44-4222, fax: 44-4333; Malé, tel: 33-2287, fax: 31-4875.
Kudahithi Relais, tel: 44-4613, fax: 44-1992; Malé, tel: 31-3938, fax: 31-3939.
Kurumba Village, tel: 44-2324, fax: 44-3885; Malé, tel: 32-3080, fax: 32-0274.

Lhohifushi, tel: 44-3451, fax: 44-1908; Malé, tel: 31-2106, fax: 32-4783.
Mahureva, tel: 44-2078, fax: 44-5941; Malé, tel: 32-3441, fax: 32-2964.
Makunudhoo, tel: 44-6464, fax: 44-6565; Malé, tel: 32-4658, fax: 32-5543.
Meeru (Meerufenfushi), tel: 44-3157, fax: 44-5946; Malé, tel: 31-4049, fax: 31-4150.
One and Only Reethi Rah, contact Maldives Tourism Promotion Board (see Useful Contacts below).
Paradise Island, tel: 44-0011, fax: 44-0022; Malé, tel: 31-6161, fax: 31-4565.
Soneva Gili, tel: 44-0304, fax: 44-0305; Malé, tel: 32-5529, fax: 32-1026.
Summer Island, tel: 44-3088, fax: 44-1910, Malé, tel: 32-2212, fax: 31-8057.
Taj Coral, tel: 44-1948, fax: 44-3884; Malé, tel: 31-7530, fax: 31-4059.
Thulhaagiri, tel: 44-5930, fax: 44-5939; Malé, tel: 32-2844, fax: 32-1026.

All resorts have at least one restaurant and a coffee shop.

Maldives Tourism Promotion Board (MTPB), Aage Building, 3rd Floor, 12 Boduthakurufaanu Magu, Malé 2004, tel: 32-3228, fax: 32-3229, www.visitmaldives.com e-mail: mtpb@visitmaldives.com

6
South Malé Atoll

Separated from North Malé by the 300m (984ft) deep Vaadhoo Channel, South Malé Atoll is approximately 30km (19 miles) long. The resorts are concentrated mostly along its eastern rim. Transport to the southern resorts is by speedboat or seaplane as it can take up to four hours to cover the same distance by motorized *dhoni*. Away from the busy waters that surround Malé and the airport, South Malé Atoll is more tranquil and it is only from the resorts of Laguna Beach (Velassaru), Vaadhoo and Taj Exotica Resort and Spa that the capital's skyline can still be seen. From the other resorts the view is one of expanses of turquoise-blue waters alternating with deep blue sea and peppered with small fishing villages and a few deserted islands.

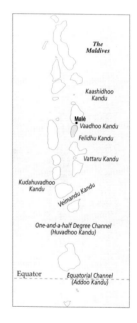

RESORT ISLANDS

As already mentioned, the islands look very similar and the lifestyle is also much the same, so to pick a resort is rather difficult. Your choice may be influenced by the amount of luxuries offered by a resort, or lack thereof – maybe you would prefer a more simple or quiet environment. Island excursions and water sports offered and nightlife may also influence your decision. Travel agencies of different countries do not offer packages to all the resorts in South Malé or on other atolls, thus limiting your choice even further.

For the food connoisseurs, remember that the quality and variety of food in the luxury resorts is generally superior to that in budget resorts.

Opposite: *Vaadhoo has a superb shallow reef just off the water bungalows. Here a snorkeller can come face to face with turtles and small blacktip reef sharks.*

DON'T MISS

*** Snorkelling: you don't have to be a scuba diver to enjoy the spectacular underwater world, and even if you have never snorkelled before – try it! Maldives is the perfect place to learn and you will be hooked.
** Fishing Villages: a trip to a local fishing island is worthwhile and will give you an insight into the lifestyles of local inhabitants. You will find that prices of the souvenirs at the fishing islands are cheaper than those at the resort.
** Malé Shopping: the trip is enjoyable and the shopping is great. There are many shops to choose from where you are sure to find a bargain!

Biyaadoo *

The island is 35km (22 miles) south of the airport, just inside the eastern rim of the atoll. Transfer from the airport takes either two and a half hours by *dhoni*, one hour by speedboat or 10 minutes by helicopter.

Lining the beach are 96 rooms set in six two-storey blocks. You can enjoy all the standard island sports and water recreations but you can also water-ski, go on banana boat rides and parasail. A boat also travels three times a day to Biyaadoo's sister island, Vilivaru.

Biyaadoo is large – 10ha (25 acres) in size. Its perimeter offers diverse settings from wide beaches to quiet enclaves with leaning palm trees. In the interior, an 880m-long (2887ft) path takes you through well-tended gardens and forests of palm trees to the accommodation. The island has its own hydroponics garden growing vegetables for the hotel's restaurant. Not relying on imported groceries, the freshly picked garden produce ensures that crisp and fresh vegetables reach the tables daily.

Nights come alive with discos, Sri Lankan fire limbos or magician shows. But it is for the diving that people will choose to spend time here, and with six marked entry points the house reef is surely one of the most spectacular.

Bolifushi **

The island is situated on the northwestern rim of the atoll, and is just 14km (9 miles) from the airport. A motorized *dhoni* takes one hour, if you go by speedboat it takes 30 minutes.

Bolifushi is small with 55 medium-range bungalows. All have air conditioning and hot and cold water. There is a restaurant, bar and disco to keep you busy when you are not scuba diving, snorkelling, water-skiing or enjoying the standard excursions available.

Cocoa Island (Maakunufushi) ★★★

Situated just inside the eastern rim of the atoll, 28km (17 miles) south of the airport, transfer is one hour by speedboat. This is a very exclusive and small resort with six water villas and 17 *dhoni*-style accommodations with elegant bedrooms, a private verandah, wooden walkways and a whirlpool. There is also a water-sports centre, a dive centre, gym, and a Shambhala retreat.

Cocoa is a beautiful, small island blessed with a lovely beach and inviting lagoon. Recreations and excursions are standard but it is a very high-range resort for those that want to be pampered.

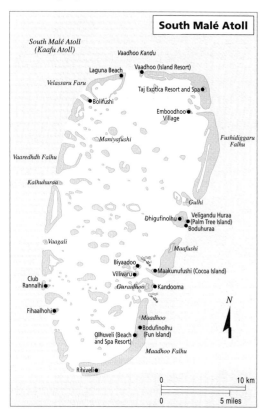

South Malé Atoll

South Malé Atoll
(Kaafu Atoll)
Vaadhoo Kandu
Laguna Beach
Vaadhoo (Island Resort)
Velassaru Faru
Taj Exotica Resort and Spa
Bolifushi
Emboodhoo
Village
Maniyafushi
Fushidiggaru
Falhu
Vaaredhdh Falhu
Kalhuhuraa
Gulhi
Veligandu Huraa
Dhigufinolhu
(Palm Tree Island)
Boduhuraa
Vaagali
Maafushi
Biyaadoo
Villivaru
Maakunufushi (Cocoa Island)
Club
Rannalhi
Guraidhoo
Kandooma
Fihaalhohi
N
Maadhoo
Bodufinolhu
Olhuveli (Beach
(Fun Island)
and Spa Resort)
Maadhoo Falhu
Rihiveli
0   10 km
0   5 miles

Above: *Paradise – is it not a leaning palm tree over clear waters, a cocktail in hand and a gently swaying swing?*
Opposite: *Set in lush, tropical vegetation, the two-storey accommodation blocks are hardly noticeable on Biyaadoo Island.*

NAUTICO DIVING CENTRE

The Nautico Watersports International Centre on **Biyaadoo** is a five-star PADI Dive School. The centre is surrounded by small locker columns where divers can store their equipment and there is enough space to hang wet suits and BCs under the coconut trees. Diving trips are flexible. Depending on the number of people, boats leave at 07:00 and return at 18:00. Diving on the house reef starts at 06:00 and night dives are possible up to 21:00.

Above: *Learn to scuba dive in the largest swimming pool on earth in the most relaxed conditions you could wish for!*

PHOTOGRAPHY

Equip yourself with everything you need before going to the islands, as you may not find the correct film or stocks may be sold out.
A few phototips:
Sunlight becomes very sharp during the day in the tropics. For softer, warmer tones the best time to shoot is during the first few hours of the morning and late afternoon to sunset. Use a polarizer to cut out the glare. Wide-angle lenses are great, especially if you can position yourself over the shallow reef, where the waters are usually very still.

Dhigufinolhu **

Dhigufinolhu is 19km (12 miles) from the airport, on the eastern rim of South Malé Atoll and transfer takes one hour by *dhoni* or 20 minutes by speedboat. It's a long and narrow island with 100 bungalows – all have air conditioning.

This is a medium- to high-range resort and facilities include a restaurant, coffee shop, bar, curio shop that sells film, snacks, T-shirts, books, postcards and souvenirs. You can play badminton and volleyball or spend most of your time in the water scuba diving, snorkelling, windsurfing, catamaran sailing and water-skiing. Excursions are standard and include a day shopping trip to Malé. There is also a connection by walkway to **Palm Tree Islands Resort** (*see* p.84).

Taj Exotica Resort and Spa (Emboodhoo Finolhu) ***

Emboodhoo Finolhu was recently redeveloped by the International Taj group who also run Taj Coral Reef in North Malé Atoll. The Taj Exotica is situated on the northern part of South Malé Atoll, just 8,5 km (5,3 miles) and a 30-minute boat transfer from the international airport. The island is long and thin, just a remarkable 12 metres wide in some places, with accommodation in 64 rooms. Most of the rooms are built on stilts over the shallow lagoon. Rooms are spaciously stylish and have hot and cold water, a mini bar, hair dryer and IDD telephone. Each room has a deck area with seating and a small ladder leading down to the sea. The island has lovely beaches, an elegant dive centre and luxury spa.

Emboodhoo Village **

Emboodhoo Village is oval-shaped and much bigger than nearby Taj Exotica. The distance to the island and mode of transport are the same. The island boasts 124 bungalows and water villas with air conditioning and hot and cold water. The restaurant serves good food and the bar and coffee shop are very sociable. The staff at the resort organize entertainment every night. There are facilities for table tennis and badminton and you can always arrange a game of volleyball on the beach. Water sports are standard but the snorkelling is particularly good as there is an excellent house reef. Excursions may be booked at reception and include a day trip to Malé shopping, island-hopping, swimming and fishing.

Fihaalhohi *

The island lies 28km (17 miles) southwest of the airport, on the western rim of the atoll. To arrive at your destination takes two and a half hours by *dhoni* or one hour by speedboat. Fihaalhohi is 450m (1476ft) long and 270m (887ft) wide which is rather small but it only has 128 rooms. All the rooms have telephones and fresh water. Facilities on the island include a restaurant, snack bar, bistro/café, bar, beach bar, shops and a disco. Light entertainment is provided.

Sports include badminton. Water sports are standard but they also offer banana boat riding and water-skiing. Excursions: Malé shopping, island-hopping trips, aerial photoflips, fishing and 'Robinson Crusoe' day trips where you can spend a day alone on a deserted island. The resort is set in lush vegetation and the island is surrounded by a good house reef easily accessible from the beach. The relaxed atmosphere and easy-going feeling is appropriate for families with children.

WATER SPORTS

Scuba diving is offered at all resorts. **Snorkelling** can be done from the beach on most islands. Otherwise, if the island doesn't have a good house reef, the resort management organizes at least two boat trips a day to reefs (free of charge depending on the resort). Most islands have a **water-sports centre** that hires equipment as well as having staff who will teach you. **Windsurfing** and **catamaran sailing** are activities that can be enjoyed on many resort islands. Water-skiing, parasailing and banana boat riding are not offered at all resorts as some have opted not to have motorized water sports to preserve the tranquil atmosphere of the island. All this may change according to the current owners and management of the water-sports facilities. It is advisable to check what is available on the island you intend visiting before you book your holiday to avoid disappointment when you get there.

Left: *Diving trips take on a relaxed atmosphere. The boats chug along over calm waters giving divers time to get ready for their dive.*

Above: *A top-of-the-range resort island, Laguna Beach offers all sorts of luxuries including a stunning pool and pool bar.*

Fun Island Resort (Bodufinolhu) ★

The resort is 38km (24 miles) south of the Hulhule International Airport, on the eastern rim of South Malé Atoll. To arrive at the island will take about three hours by *dhoni* or 45 minutes by speedboat.

Fun Island Resort is long and narrow; it has a length of 800m (2625ft) but it is only 30m (98ft) at its widest point. 100 rooms line the beach, each with air conditioning, hot and cold fresh water, mini bar and telephone. It's a bit of a squeeze but the atmosphere is great. Fun Island has three bars – one of which has a wooden deck stretching over the lagoon. There are shops and a disco and an intimate *à la carte* restaurant and a main dining room that serves sumptuous buffets. All beach and water sports are standard activities although you can also water-ski.

The excursions offered are Malé shopping, island-hopping, fishing, a barbecue night and walks to two uninhabited islands close enough to reach at low tide.

Kandooma ★

Kandooma is situated 30km (19 miles) south of the airport, on the eastern rim of the atoll. The *dhoni* transfer takes three hours, the speedboat takes 45 minutes and if you are fortunate enough to have been able to book in advance for the helicopter, it will be about 10 minutes' flying time. There are 102 simple bungalows and some have air conditioning as well as hot and cold water. The resort has a restaurant, bar and disco as it is a budget-range resort but it does offer banana riding and badminton. Water sports are standard and you can water-ski or go on excursions.

Laguna Beach (Velassaru) ★★★

The resort is about 11km (7 miles) southwest of the airport on the northern rim of South Malé Atoll near Vaadhoo Channel. Transfer from the airport is approximately one hour by *dhoni* or 30 minutes by speedboat.

This is a medium-sized island in the high-range with 129 luxury cottages that all have a sea view. The main restaurant serves good food, the Four Seasons serves Western cuisine and the Dragon Inn specializes in Chinese food. It has an international coffee shop, open barbecue terrace and bar. Gymnasium, shops, disco and a lovely freshwater pool with a rocky water feature and a pool bar are available for the enjoyment and convenience of discerning guests. Being so close to Malé, there are regular shopping excursions to the capital city and you can also enjoy island-hopping and fishing trips. Close to the **Vaadhoo Channel's** best dive sites and with a good house reef, Laguna offers a luxurious hideaway on a lush island with fine beaches and a picture-book pretty lagoon.

Olhuveli Beach and Spa Resort ✦✦✦

The resort is set in an expansive turquoise lagoon. Water bungalows resembling little pink boxes on stilts rather than tropical holiday accommodation are set in the shallow lagoon. A Japanese company has recently spent US$ 17 million on this development. On the eastern rim of South Malé Atoll, Olhuveli is 39km (24 miles) to the south of the airport. Transfer takes three hours by *dhoni*, one hour by speedboat or 20 minutes if you have made prior arrangements to fly.

The island is long and narrow and has 125 rooms set in two-storey apartments and a series of water villas.

There is a bar, freshwater swimming pool, shops, spa and a disco. You can play tennis and mini golf or enjoy the standard water sports. The resort has a reputation for big-game fishing. At low tide you can stroll to the nearby uninhabited island.

NEW RESORTS

In 2004 the Maldivian government announced that 11 new resorts and one new hotel are to be developed. It will take about 2–3 years for most of them to open but when they do, tourism will be established in every atoll of the Maldives. The new resorts will include the following:
Haa Alifu Atoll, Alidhoo
Haa Dhaalu Atoll, Hondaafushi
Shaviyani Atoll, Dholhiyadhoo
Noonu Atoll, Maavelavaru
Noonu Atoll, Randheli
Thaa Atoll, Kalhufahalafushi
Laamu Atoll, Olhuveli
Gaafu Alifu Atoll, Hadahaa
Gaafu Dhaalu Atoll, Funamadhua
Gaafu Dhaalu Atoll, Konotta
Gaafu Dhaalu Atoll, Lonudhuahutta
Gnaviyani Atoll, Foammulah

Below: *Olhuveli's water villas resemble little boxes adrift on the water.*

Palm Tree Islands Resort ***

Palm Tree Island (Veligandu Huraa) is situated 20km (12 miles) south of the airport, on the eastern rim of the atoll, so the journey to this high-range resort takes one hour by *dhoni* or 20 minutes by speedboat. The size of the island is very small – with 56 thatched, luxurious bungalows. Each suite has air conditioning, hot and cold water and a telephone. The restaurant, situated in the centre of the small island, is in the open air and surrounded by palm trees.

Island activities are badminton and table tennis and you can scuba dive, snorkel, windsurf, sail a catamaran and water-ski. Excursions are standard.

Palm Tree Island is part of a group of three resort islands that are connected by a wooden jetty. At the junction of the three jetties is a small bar. The other islands are **Dhigufinolhu** and the new resort, **Boduhuraa**. Another island holds the dive school, staff quarters of Palm Tree Island as well as all the generators and the desalinization plant. These noisy machines have thoughtfully been kept away from the guests in an attempt to maintain the peace and tranquillity that the Maldive islands are known for.

Club Rannalhi ***

Rannalhi is 27km (17 miles) from the airport, on the western rim of the atoll. It takes two hours by *dhoni* or 45 minutes by speedboat to arrive at the island. The size of Rannalhi is about 4ha (10 acres) and there are 116 deluxe rooms, including 16 water bungalows built on stilts over the lagoon. Meals are taken at the restaurant and there is a bar, shop and disco. The beach games, water sports and excursions on offer are standard, and the snorkelling is excellent.

BIRD WATCHING

Maldives does not have large numbers of species, infact, it sometimes seems remarkably devoid of birds. However, for the dedicated birder there is still much of interest. November is the best month for northern winter migrants, so a resort stay at this time could be particularly rewarding. **Addu Atoll** in the far south is probably the best single location for birding both because several islands are linked by causeways making it easy to travel about independently and because there are accessible brackish and fresh-water lakes. For seabirds, there are no dedicated pelagic trips, but liveaboard whale and dolphin watching cruises invariably turn up plenty of goodies.

Rihiveli ★★★

This 3.5ha (9 acre) beach resort is about 50km (31 miles) south of Hulhule International Airport and is the south-ernmost resort of South Malé Atoll. Transfers from the airport take over one hour by speedboat. Rihiveli boasts 48 newly refurbished bungalows with hot and cold fresh water. The chef ensures a wonderful selection of excellent food, the sunset bar contains a games room, shop, library and billiard room. Sports are beach volleyball, half-court tennis, petanque, table tennis, basketball, aerobics and weights. Water sports offered are (free) snorkelling by boat, water-skiing, windsurfing, catamaran sailing and canoeing. Scuba diving, parasailing and night snorkelling can be arranged for a small fee. Free half- and full-day excursions, picnics, fishing and bivouac (two days and one night on a safari *dhoni*) can be organized from the reception on the island. Deep-sea fishing (extra charge), Malé shopping and aerial photoflips are other options. This natural island has a distinct French ambience. Wait for low tide and you can wade to two small uninhabited islands.

Vaadhoo Island Resort ★★

Vaadhoo has given its name to the deep **Vaadhoo Channel** that separates Kaafu (North and South Malé) Atoll. It is 8km (5 miles) from the airport and, because of its position, offers outstanding marine life. Transfer from the airport takes an hour by *dhoni* or 20 minutes if you are travelling by speedboat. The size of the island is so small that it only takes about five minutes to stroll around it! Hence, there are only 33 rooms grouped in two-storey flats on the

Opposite: *Windsurfing can be enjoyed even by the inexperienced sportsman.*
Above: *Vaadhoo Island is surrounded by a fantastic house reef which is regularly visited by pelagic species.*
Below: *The Vaadhoo water bungalows are the epitome of seaside, island living.*

Above: *Vaadhoo's prized possession are the seven water villas that make up the sunset wing of the accommodation on this tiny resort island.*

sunrise wing and seven water villas on the sunset wing over the lagoon. All have air conditioning and hot and cold water. Vaadhoo's prized possession are the seven stunning Maldivian-style water villas built of wood, bamboo and palm leaves. Inside, the bath tub is flanked by a large window that faces onto the lagoon, while in the spacious bedroom, the coffee table resembles a transparent skylight that allows one to see corals, fish, turtles, blacktip reef sharks and other inhabitants of the lagoon below.

A wonderful, 'floating' bar and another one for those who prefer terra firma, a restaurant and shop provide the pampering the guests look forward to after a hard day of scuba diving, snorkelling, windsurfing and catamaran sailing. Excursions that may be booked at reception include Malé shopping, island-hopping, aerial photoflips and fishing trips.

Vilivaru **

Biyaadoo's sister island offers the same facilities in quieter surroundings. The diving is just as exciting and the snorkelling on the house reef superb. The island is 35km (22 miles) from the airport, just inside the atoll's eastern rim. Transfer takes either two and a half hours by *dhoni*, one hour by speedboat or 10 minutes if you have arranged to fly. Vilivaru is about 5ha (12 acres) in size and has 60 bungalows. Each one is equipped with air conditioning, hot and cold fresh water, a mini bar and telephone. Incidentally, the food is excellent. Apart from all the standard resort recreations, excursions and facilities, there are three daily transfers to Vilivaru's sister island, Biyaadoo.

VAADHOO DIVING CLUB

The dive school is strategically placed on the jetty near the diving *dhonis*. The management, being extremely concerned about the underwater environment, insists that divers dive with no gloves thereby ensuring that they look and think before carelessly touching anything. The dive sites offered are the best in the area. Snorkelling and diving along the 30m (98ft) drop-off gives the casual observer and divers a good chance of seeing **eagle rays**, **turtles** and **blacktip reef sharks**.

South Malé Atoll at a Glance

BEST TIME TO VISIT

From about **November** through to **April** the weather is usually hot and the skies bright blue. The water is warm throughout the year and the sea is also calm during these months which is an important consideration if you are planning a snorkelling or scuba diving holiday. This is certainly the best time to visit Maldives although the islands are an all-year-round destination. During the wetter months between **May** and **October** the days are often broken by storms and humid tropical showers.

GETTING THERE

Flying is the quickest and best option to get to Maldives. Regular charter and national airlines connect the capital, Malé, to all continents. The only way to get to **Malé** from **Hulhule** International Airport is by water taxi/*dhoni*. There are many water taxis going to and fro on a continuous basis and the crossing takes about 10 minutes.

GETTING AROUND

If you have booked a package holiday to a resort, an island representative will meet you at the airport and ensure you reach your destination. Resort islands have their own boats to transport passengers – usually motorized *dhonis* or speedboats. There are two sea plane companies.

WHERE TO STAY

Resort islands are scattered within the atoll. They are similar in size and the recreations offered. Style and standard of facilities and accommodation varies greatly from luxury, mid-range to budget.

Bodu Huraa, tel: 44-0172.
Biyaadoo, tel: 44-7171, fax: 44-7272; Malé, tel: 32-4699, fax: 32-7014.
Bolifushi, tel: 44-3517, fax: 44-5924; Malé, tel: 31-7526, fax: 31-7529.
Club Rannalhi, tel: 44-2688, fax: 44-2035; Malé, tel: 32-3323, fax: 31-7993.
Cocoa Island, tel: 44-1818, fax: 44-1919; Malé, tel: 32-5529, fax: 31-8992.
Dhigufinolhu, tel: 44-3599, fax: 44-3886; Malé, tel: 31-4008, fax: 32-7058.
Emboodhoo Village, tel: 44-4776, fax: 44-2673; Malé, tel: 32-2212, fax: 31-8057.
Fihaalhoni, tel: 44-2903, fax: 44-3803; Malé, tel: 32-3369, fax: 32-4752.
Fun Island Resort (Bodufinolhu), tel: 44-4558, fax: 44-3958; Malé, tel: 31-6161, fax: 31-4565.
Kandooma Tourist Resort, tel: 44-4452, fax: 44-5948; Malé, tel: 32-3360, fax: 32-6880.
Laguna Beach (Velassaru), tel: 44-5903, fax: 44-3041; Malé, tel: 32-3080, fax: 32-2674.
Maakunufushi (Cocoa Island), tel: 44-3713, fax: 44-1919;

Malé, tel: 32-5528, fax: 31-8992.
Olhuveli, tel: 44-1957, fax: 44-5942; Malé, tel: 31-3646, fax: 31-3644.
Palm Tree Island (Veligandu Huraa), tel: 44-3882, fax: 44-0009; Malé, tel: 31-4008, fax: 32-7058.
Rihiveli Beach Resort, tel: 44-1994, fax: 44-0052; Malé, tel: 32-8422, fax: 31-8405.
Taj Exotica, tel: 44-2200, www.tajhotels.com/maldives
Vaadhoo Island Resort, tel: 44-3976, fax: 44-3397; Malé, tel: 32-5844, fax: 32-5846.
Vilivaru, tel: 44-7070, fax: 44-7272; Malé, tel: 32-4699, fax: 32-7014.

WHERE TO EAT

All resorts have at least one restaurant. For resorts that have more than one restaurant it is advisable to book a half-board package instead of full board, giving you the flexibility of changing restaurants.

TOURS AND EXCURSIONS

These are usually booked on a daily basis from the reception. It is advisable to make a reservation a day in advance. Excursions are standard on most islands and range from diving, to island-hopping and trips to the capital, Malé.

USEFUL CONTACTS

Maldives Tourism Promotion Board, *see* Useful Contacts, page 57.

7
Ari and Felidhu Atolls

Separated from North and South Malé (Kaafu) Atolls by the deep **Alihuras Kandu**, Ari Atoll is part of the western chain of Maldives' turquoise necklace. At first, the government was reluctant to allow resorts to be developed in this area, however, there are now 26 operating resorts.

Ari Atoll is oval-shaped and is 80km (50 miles) long and 30km (19 miles) wide. To its northeast there are two small satellite atolls which form part of Ari Atoll: **Rasdhoo** and **Thoddoo Atolls**. The round atoll of Rasdhoo has three islands, two of which are resorts and the third a fishing village.

Shaped like a boot, **Felidhu Atoll** is situated south of South Malé Atoll, across the 20km-wide (12-mile) **Felidhoo Kandu Channel**. Felidhu lies 66km (41 miles) south from the capital city of Malé which is in North Malé Atoll. It is quiet and has only five inhabited islands and two resort islands.

ARI (ALIFU) ATOLL RESORT ISLANDS

The best and quickest way to travel to the resort islands of **Ari Atoll** is by seaplane. Not only is this an enjoyable scenic route, crossing over the southern part of North Malé and the northern part of South Malé, but it also avoids crossing the 40km-wide (25-mile) **Alihuras Kandu** by speedboat (a ride that sometimes proves to be rather bumpy). Having spent considerable time in an air-craft already, most visitors choose resorts that do not require too much travelling time to reach.

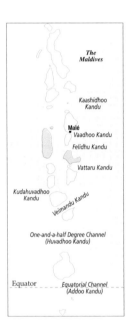

The Maldives

Kaashidhoo Kandu

Malé
Vaadhoo Kandu

Felidhu Kandu

Vattaru Kandu

Kudahuvadhoo Kandu

Veimandu Kandu

One-and-a-half Degree Channel
(Huvadhoo Kandu)

Equator   Equatorial Channel
(Addoo Kandu)

Opposite: *Ranveli is a popular island among Italians. The sparkling pool is set overlooking a turquoise lagoon.*

Right: *Angaga is a quiet island located within the rim of the Ari Atoll. Here buildings and bungalows are hidden among the lush vegetation.*
Opposite: *White Sands Resort, like most other Maldivian resorts, offers beautiful white beaches and a variety of water sports.*

MEALS IN MALDIVES

Maldives is not an agricultural nation. The infertile islands yield the bare minimum for the locals, and that, sometimes, is not enough! With an abundant supply of only coconuts and fish, Maldives import almost everything else, especially for the resort islands. Fish, usually tuna, is generally served at every meal, while the main carbohydrate is rice. The better hotels serve sumptuous meals, and you may even have a choice of restaurants. At luxury resorts you will have a wide variety of foods, so it's more expensive. However, at the more economical, budget resorts and those that are further away from the airport, you may have to endure basic fare and a 'mixed salad' of different cabbages when supplies are low!
The best way to experience true Maldivian cuisine is by visiting a local café.

Angaga ★★
Angaga is a quiet island and appeals to those who prefer a peaceful holiday. It is very popular and always has a mixture of nationalities. It is situated about 90km (56 miles) southwest of the airport, in the centre of the southern Ari Atoll. The transfer takes about two and a half hours by speedboat and about 30 minutes by seaplane.

A small island with a large, moving sand bank, Angaga has 50 thatched bungalows with air conditioning and hot and cold water. Nestled in the thick vegetation, the discreet rooms seem to have been haphazardly scattered around the perimeter of the island to avoid uprooting existing trees. Maldivian swings adorn the sandy veranda of each room. The bar and restaurant have been placed side by side with roofs shaped like two jumping dolphins and there is an excellent coffee shop on the island. The tiny gift shop also sells suntan lotion and snacks, books, fabric and film.

Volleyball and badminton are popular and water sports offered are scuba diving, snorkelling, sailing on catamarans, water-skiing, windsurfing and parasailing. The resort offers half- and full-day excursions like trips to Malé and island-hopping. Fishing trips are also arranged. Snorkelling trips are conducted regularly by *dhoni* to **Pineapple Island**, a nearby uninhabited island with pristine coral gardens, that is leased by the resort for the use of its patrons.

White Sands Resort (Dhidhdhoofinolhu) ★★★

This resort island lies 104km (65 miles) southwest of the airport on the southern rim of the Ari Atoll and the trip is about two and a half hours by speedboat and 35 minutes by seaplane. The resort is 1.7km (1 mile) long and 300m (328yd) wide with 141 standard and medium A-frame bungalows. There is an island village and a water village. The mid-range rooms have air conditioning, hot and cold water and a mini bar. The facilities include a restaurant, bar, shops and a disco. Tennis, table tennis, badminton, soccer and volleyball are offered on land while scuba diving, snorkelling, catamaran sailing, windsurfing, canoeing, water-skiing and parasailing are the water-sports options. Half- and full-day excursions, aerial photoflips and fishing trips can be arranged at the reception. The house reef is too far for people to swim to, so daily boat trips are organized to good snorkelling spots.

Athuruga ★

The small all-inclusive resort island of Athuruga is 68km (42 miles) southwest of the airport on the eastern rim of the Ari Atoll. If the weather is fine, it should take two hours by speedboat and 20 minutes flying. At the moment there are 46 bungalows with air conditioning and hot and cold water. There is a restaurant, bar and shop and volleyball and table tennis are popular with tourists. Water sports are standard while daily excursions can be arranged at the reception.

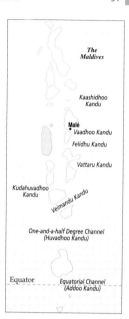

THODDOO ISLAND

To the north of the small round **Rasdhoo Atoll**, there is a single island that rises from the ocean deep – **Thoddoo**. This island is well known among the locals for its **watermelon plantations** and its **dancing women**. As on many other Maldivian islands, Thoddoo is littered with the remains of **Buddhist** temples. During an excavation, a complete sculpture of Buddha was found in a hidden chamber together with **silver** and **gold** artefacts and two **coins**, one of which seems to have been minted in Rome in AD90.

Bathala *

Almost 58km (36 miles) west of the airport on the eastern rim of Ari Atoll, the transfer to Bathala takes either three and a half hours by *dhoni*, 90 minutes by speedboat or 20 minutes by seaplane. Then you board a *dhoni* for the short trip to the island.

Bathala is oval-shaped and very small. It is a medium- and budget-range resort with 37 thatched, air-conditioned bungalows. There is a restaurant, bar, spa and you can play volleyball or badminton. Half- and full-day excursions, aerial photoflips and fishing trips are offered. The island is geared towards the diving fraternity. It is surrounded by a beautiful **house reef** that drops off to the floor of the nearby channel.

Ellaidhoo *

This small but spacious island is 57km (36 miles) west of the airport, on the eastern rim of the Ari Atoll. Transfer from the airport is 90 minutes by air-conditioned speedboat. There are 78 thatched, simple bungalows, built on wooden platforms lining the beach. Each has an air conditioner, TV, hot and cold water and a Maldivian-style bathroom opening onto a private garden. There is also a gym and massage centre. Food is served in an open-air restaurant and the bar has alcohol and soft drinks. Soccer, volleyball and badminton are the usual sports and the island has catamarans and windsurfers for hire. Snorkelling and diving are the main attraction, and the staff also arrange half-and full-day excursions and fishing outings.

Right: *Ellaidhoo is perfect for diving as it is surrounded by a stunning house reef.*

Fesdu Fun Island (Fesdhoo) ★★

It takes about 30 minutes to walk around the island but it doesn't feel small. It is 64km (40 miles) from the airport, inside Ari Atoll. You will travel for 2½ hours by air-conditioned speedboat or 25 minutes by seaplane. Accommodation is in 50 quaint bungalows which have hot and cold water. Air conditioning is available for an additional supplement. This mid-range resort has a restaurant, bar and sun deck. Island sports and water sports are standard activities. Excursions are arranged on request at the reception. Fesdu's best feature is its stunning surrounding, wide, sandy beach and the equally exciting **house reef**.

Gangehi
Island Resort ★★★

About 60km (37 miles) west on the northern rim of Ari Atoll, transfer from the airport takes about two hours by speed launch or 25 minutes by seaplane. This is an exclusive and expensive resort with 25 luxury bungalows. Air conditioning, hot and cold water, a telephone, fridge, hairdryer and safety deposit box are standard. Facilities include a smart restaurant, piano bar, medical centre and shops. Scuba diving, snorkelling and canoeing are the only sports, but excursions are arranged (no deep-sea fishing). Gangehi is a small and elegant island for those who prefer a quiet holiday.

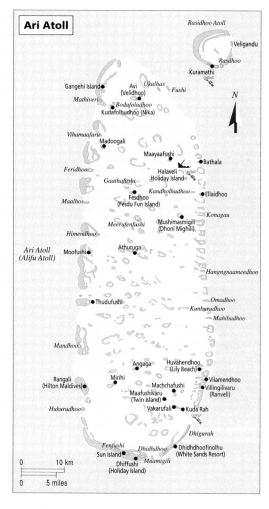

CALYPSO DIVING CENTRE

The well-organized dive school on **Holiday Island** has air-conditioned lecture rooms, a cool storage room for guests' equipment and its own jetty. The less energetic diver will be pleased to know that attentive staff fetch your equipment from your room and carry all equipment on and off the diving *dhonis* before and after the dive trips (do tip the staff). Diving in the south Ari Atoll offers a variety of experiences including the chance to dive with **whale sharks** between the months of October and December.

Opposite: *Holiday Island has 142 modern, luxury rooms that line the beach.*
Below: *The wooden deck of the bar on Holiday Island is the perfect place for an exotic sundowner.*

Halaveli Holiday Island ★★

A medium-range resort set on a beautiful island with a wide beach and large lagoon, Halaveli Holiday Island is popular with divers. It is 55km (34 miles) from the airport, inside Ari Atoll. The crossing is generally by speedboat and takes two hours.

The island is only 700m (2300ft) in diameter and there are 56 thatched bungalows with air conditioning, hot and cold water and a fridge. Water sports offered are scuba diving, snorkelling, catamaran sailing, windsurfing, canoeing and water-skiing. Staff may also arrange excursions.

Holiday Island (Dhiffushi) ★★★

An unusually large and long island on the southern rim of Ari Atoll, Holiday Island is 110km (68 miles) southwest of Hulhule. Your travel agent will probably arrange transfer by speedboat which takes two hours.

Guests stay in one of the 142 modern, luxury and spacious bungalows with air conditioning, hot and cold water, a telephone (even in the bathroom!), hairdryer, and television. The restaurant serves the most sumptuous buffets for breakfast, lunch and dinner; a bar with a wooden deck stretches over the lagoon; and a curio shop, photographic shop and jewellery shop as well as a small gymnasium with sauna are all at the convenience of the tourist. There is a tennis court and table tennis, volleyball and badminton facilities. Water sports to enjoy are scuba diving, snorkelling, catamaran sailing, windsurfing, water-skiing and canoeing. Half- and full-day excursions, aerial photoflips, fishing and free snorkelling safaris may be booked at the reception desk.

The extensive grounds of this new resort have been cleared of undergrowth and well-raked, sandy floors alternate with colourful gardens – all under a canopy of tall palm trees. Lovely beaches encircle the island with the water-sport school on the sand bank at its west end. Holiday Island's lagoon is well suited for windsurfing enthusiasts who can catch the wind from whichever way it blows and still stay within the calm and protective waters of the lagoon.

Kuda Rah ★★★

Kuda Rah is a small, intimate island 95km (60 miles) southwest of the airport. It is inside Ari Atoll at its southern end and the trip takes approximately two hours by boat or 30 minutes flying. One of the most exclusive resorts in Maldives, it has only 25 spacious bungalows with a lounge and five water villas. All have air conditioning, hot and cold water, a telephone, mini bar, private safe and television. Facilities are top of the range with an excellent restaurant, bar, sea water swimming pool, shop and medical staff available. The tennis court has floodlights and the snooker tables are full-size. Water sports on offer are scuba diving, snorkelling on an excellent house reef and canoeing. Free daily excursions are arranged to neighbouring islands and fishing trips are offered at extra cost.

Lily Beach (Huvahendhoo) ★★★

This all-inclusive, mid-range resort has a freshwater swimming pool, gymnasium and tennis court. Island-hopping and snorkelling safaris are a daily option. A visit to a nearby fishing village can also be arranged.

Lily Beach is 71km (44 miles) southwest of the airport, on the eastern rim of Ari Atoll. Transfers take about two hours by speedboat or 30 minutes by seaplane. The island is 550m (1805ft) long and 100m (328ft) wide which means that you step out of your suite onto

---

TRANSFERS TO ISLANDS

You travel to your paradise island either by motorized *dhoni*, **speedboat** or **seaplane**. The mode of transport is usually arranged when you book your package tour, and if you select to fly, it costs more as running costs are so expensive. Some travel agencies arrange air transfers as part of the price of the package tour offered. Islands close to the airport usually use a motorized *dhoni* to transfer visitors to their resort island but this mode of transport would be much too slow when travelling to outlying islands situated far away, so most resorts use speedboats. Bring along tablets if you suffer from motion sickness.

Opposite: *A few resort islands have speedboats for fishing that make trips to the deep seas outside the atoll.*
Below: *Traditional fishing dhonis are available for those who would prefer to fish Maldivian style.*

the beach. The island boasts 84 superior rooms with air conditioning, hot and cold water, a hairdryer, mini bar, private wooden sun deck, sitting area and an open-air bathroom – Maldivian-style. The restaurant offers a wide range of Western and Maldivian food and the coffee shop serves delicious snacks. Nightlife is enlivened with a disco and fully stocked bar and you can always spend a few hours playing table tennis. Outdoor activities include tennis, volleyball, scuba diving, snorkelling over a good house reef and windsurfing. Excursions are the same as offered at most resorts.

Maayaafushi **

This small round island is 60km (40 miles) southwest of the airport, just inside the eastern rim of Ari Atoll and it takes about two hours by speedboat or 30 minutes flying.

The lovely resort is set in tropical, lush vegetation, surrounded by a perfect beach that lends itself to the relaxing atmosphere of the resort. Perfect for divers, it is situated near some of the best diving spots of the Ari Atoll. It is a medium-range resort which is comfortable but rustic and the 60 simply furnished, Maldivian-style bungalows have recently been renovated.

Meals are usually included in the package deal made through your travel agent and are served in the restaurant. If you don't feel like eating what is set on the daily menu, you can buy filling snacks from the coffee shop. Nightlife consists of an open-air bar and lively disco. Badminton, volleyball, scuba diving, snorkelling, catamaran sailing, windsurfing, parasailing and water-skiing are activities offered and aerial photoflips, island-hopping and fishing excursions may be booked, which will cost extra.

Machchafushi ***

This small resort island is 95km (59 miles) from the airport, in the south of Ari Atoll, and the transfer takes two and a half hours by speedboat or 30 minutes flying. Arrangements for mode of transport are finalized when you book your tour. Accommodation is a string of 64 bungalows with a sea view, air conditioning, hot and cold water and a mini bar. When not snorkelling, diving, sunbathing, windsurfing or sailing catamarans, visitors can swim in the pool, play tennis or visit the shop and bar.

There are also facilities for badminton, volleyball and table tennis. Island-hopping excursions, fishing and aerial flips can be arranged at reception. A good house reef, a lovely lagoon and fine, sandy beaches encircle the small island.

Madoogali ★★★

This high-range resort, also inside Ari Atoll, is 78km (48 miles) from the airport. You travel 90 minutes by speedboat or fly 20 minutes by seaplane. It's a small island with 56 deluxe bungalows. Air conditioning, hot and cold water and a telephone are standard. Guests can join aerobic classes, spend time at the sociable bar, play table tennis, or relax in the new spa.

Water activities on the island are scuba diving, snorkelling, catamaran sailing, windsurfing, waterskiing, parasailing and canoeing. Unless you are on a special tour you will have to pay extra to hire equipment. The resort also offers island-hopping and fishing.

Mirihi ★★★

The island is 80km (50 miles) from the airport and you are flown there by seaplane. The flying time is about 30 minutes. This paradise island is 300m (984ft) long and 100m (328ft) wide, which is very small.

Consequently there are only 30 luxury water villas and eight bungalows with air conditioning, hot and cold water, a fridge and telephone.

WHAT TO WEAR

Unless you are staying at a luxury resort where there are smart, air-conditioned restaurants and an array of entertainment that lends itself to dressing up, most resorts have a **casual code of dress**. After all, you are on holiday and the last thing you would want to do is to wear a tie to dinner! Many resorts have not tiled their floors and sand flows throughout the common facilities so . . . take off your shoes as you arrive at the resort and leave them off until it is time to leave. Remember that this is a Muslim country; no nudity is allowed (you can get fined). You will not be allowed into the bar or the restaurant wearing only your bathing suit and, most importantly, when visiting a local island, respect their customs. The weather is hot and humid, so wear light cotton rather than synthetic clothing. Don't forget a hat, sunglasses and suntan lotion.

This top-of-the-range resort has the facilities that are offered on most other resort islands, but here they are more up-market. Water sports include scuba diving, excellent snorkelling, windsurfing and a few catamarans. Mirihi has a gymnasium, which is not very common on the resort islands.

Above: *Catamaran sailing is one of the many water sports offered at Mirihi Island Resort.*

ISLAND WATER

Some of the local islands have a well from which they draw brackish water. The government has started to install catchment and storage facilities for rainwater, while some islanders still collect runoff water from their roofs when it rains. In the resorts there is usually a desalinization plant. This water is fine for brushing your teeth but not for drinking. It is advisable to drink only **bottled**, **mineral water** but ensure that the bottle given to you has a sealed top. On some islands there are drinking-water taps and although it may not taste as good as the water at home, it is, nevertheless, safe to drink.

Moofushi **

Approximately 84km (52 miles) southwest of the airport inside the Ari Atoll, transfer from the airport to Moofushi is two hours by speedboat or 30 minutes flying. A small, medium- to high-range resort island with 60 bungalows and water villas, it also has a restaurant, bar, shop and disco. Volleyball, table tennis, scuba diving, snorkelling, windsurfing and canoeing are on offer, as are half- and full-day excursions, aerial photoflips and fishing.

Nika Hotel (Kudafolhudhoo) ***

The exclusive Nika Hotel was designed by an Italian architect for the privileged few. With an exorbitant room rate especially during high season, it is one of the most expensive resorts of Maldives. The hotel is 69km (43 miles) from the airport, near the northern tip of the Ari Atoll, and transfer is about two hours by speedboat or 20 minutes flying.

A small island, it boasts 26 spacious cottages that offer maximum privacy, each 70m² (230 sq ft) of total comfort with a bedroom, lounge, and Maldivian-style bathroom set in a private garden with a solarium. Ceiling fans, hot and cold water, a telephone and mini bar complete these unique living quarters. The restaurant serves excellent food and the coffee shop and bar are outstanding. Activities include tennis, bowling, badminton and volleyball, scuba diving, snorkelling, windsurfing, canoeing and water-skiing. Honeymooners have the option of being taken to a secluded, deserted island with a picnic basket and a bottle of champagne. Fishing excursions are also available.

Hilton Maldives (Rangali) ★★★

Far from the airport – 100km (62 miles) – on the western rim of Ari Atoll, transfer to Rangali is just over two and a half hours by speedboat or 35 minutes by air. Rangali Island was recently redeveloped for the Hilton group and offers a high standard of accommodation and facilities. The resort is spread across two islands that are linked by a wooden causeway. It is a large resort with 152 villas. Each has a beautiful Maldivian-style bathroom, air conditioning, hot and cold water and a mini bar.

Water sports are standard as are the excursions. If ever there was a resort that epitomizes Maldivian style while skilfully blending it with five-star luxury, it is Rangali. Clean-cut but lavish, the series of reception rooms, bars and restaurants flows easily from one to the other and spills over to the outside via retractable glass walls and sandy floors.

Ranveli Village (Villingilivaru) ★★

Southwest on the eastern rim of the Ari Atoll, this resort is 85km (53 miles) from the airport. Transfer to Ranveli takes 25 minutes by seaplane. The island looks like a small tongue emerging from an extensive coral reef. There are 56 tastefully furnished rooms set in 14 two-storey blocks. All suites have air conditioning, a fridge, hot and cold water and a telephone.

Activities are volleyball, table tennis, scuba diving, snorkelling, canoeing and windsurfing. There is a swimming pool, pool bar and medical service. Excursions are also advertized on the notice boards. Set on stilts

---

THE MALDIVIAN WAY

When you first hear that your bathroom is outside, you may be a little apprehensive but the resorts have developed a unique style of incorporating the bathroom into the room and its natural surroundings. This has commonly become known as 'Maldivian style'. An enclosed garden extends out of the back of the room. A covered and tiled area has a shower or bath, a basin and toilet. The rest is a sandy patch with several plants.

Below: *Ranveli is so small that the bar and restaurant had to be raised on stilts over the shallow lagoon.*

in the aquamarine, shallow lagoon, the bar and restaurant area is a grandiose wooden structure with a series of flowing rooms, balconies and high ceilings. Reminiscent of its Italian beginnings, the food is superb.

Sun Island Resort

This is one of the largest and most recently developed resort islands in the Maldives. Situated 100km (62 miles) from the airport in the very south of Ari Atoll, Sun Island has 350 rooms including bungalows, water bungalows and suites. All rooms have air conditioning and hot and cold water. Sports facilities are comprehensive. The island is managed by Villa Hotels who own the neighbouring Holiday Island.

Thudufushi *

Situated 75km (47 miles) southwest of the airport within the Ari Atoll, transfers take under two hours by speedboat. Thudufushi is a small 'all-inclusive' island with 47 suites. Facilities and excursions are standard, as offered on most of the other islands and there is a disco for all-night raving. Enjoy scuba diving or snorkelling, or you can hire catamarans, windsurfers and canoes.

Twin Island (Maafushivaru) ***

This is a small island 80km (50 miles) southwest of the airport in the south of Ari Atoll. Guests are flown there and it takes about 30 minutes.

Facing the sea are 38 modern, well-furnished bungalows with air conditioning and hot and cold water. Facilities and water-related acitivities offered are standard as per other resorts.

Above: *A long strip of sugar-white sand extends westward from the little island of Ranveli.*
Opposite: *Experience the 'back to nature' feel of Vilamendhoo.*

TIPPING

Porters: US$1 per piece of luggage for the porters who carry it to and from your room.
House staff: US$1 per person per day for the staff responsible for cleaning your rooms.
Waiters: US$1 per person per day for the staff serving at your table.
Excursions: US$1 per person per boat trip for the *dhoni* crew. (Scuba divers may want to give more for the boat crew who help with their kit.)
Bar service: Most bars include a service charge.

Vakarufali ★★★

This deluxe resort is just inside the eastern rim of the southern Ari Atoll and 95km (60 miles) from Hulhule. The trip takes 30 minutes flying. The 50 thatched, traditional bungalows all have air conditioning, hot and cold water, open-air bathrooms and a fridge. It's a quieter, exclusive resort. Amenities are similar to those on most islands – and you can always scuba dive and snorkel. A babysitting service is offered to visitors with children.

Velidhoo (Avi) ★★

This is a medium-range resort, 60km (37 miles) from Hulhule, on the northern tip of the Ari Atoll. The trip takes either five hours by *dhoni*, two hours by speedboat or 18 minutes by seaplane.

The island is 7ha (19 acres) and has 80 deluxe rooms with air conditioning, hot and cold fresh water and a fridge. In addition there are 20 dreamy and isolated water bungalows, some with jacuzzi. Apart from the standard facilities, the resort has a gymnasium and disco. Excursions include island-hopping, shopping in Malé and fishing. An excellent house reef is only a few swimming strokes away from the beach.

Vilamendhoo Island Resort ★★

Vilamendhoo is for the person who is prepared to give up the five-star facilities synonymous with the Western world. It is an island that brings you back to nature, where all that matters is a perfect beach-lapped by warm clear waters set against a backdrop of cool greenery.

This island is on the eastern rim of Ari Atoll, near Ranveli Beach Resort (Villingilivaru). Transfers are usually to Maafushivaru with a further half-hour by *dhoni*. When the concept of this island was first conceived, the thought was to build the Maldives' first eco-island where no

> **VILAMENDHOO'S DIVE SCHOOL**
>
> Although the dive school is new, its instructors have ample experience in Maldivian waters. The owner has been running diving operations in the Maldives for over 10 years and his instructors are all well acquainted with the territory. Twice a day three *dhonis* take divers to six different dive sites. The first *dhoni*, for more experienced scuba divers, goes to exciting spots with strong current and subsequently lots of pelagic life. The second *dhoni* concentrates on photographic expeditions and the third is for beginners and divers who prefer a more leisurely dive.

The Maldives

Kaashidhoo Kandu

Malé
Vaadhoo Kandu
Felidhu Kandu

Vattaru Kandu

Kudahuvadhoo Kandu
Veimandu Kandu

One-and-a-half Degree Channel (Huvadhoo Kandu)

Equator
Equatorial Channel (Addoo Kandu)

Opposite: *A romantic sunset view of Kuramathi and its thatched jetties.*
Below: *Vilamendhoo is one of the Maldivian resorts closest to nature.*

polluting waste would leak into the environment and all the energy would be obtained naturally. Unfortunately, the space needed for a solar plant big enough to create energy for the entire island would have taken all the land space available, so it was reluctantly decided to install a generator instead.

In building the resort and its facilities, little of the rich vegetation on the island was displaced. Sandy pathways lead into the forest of palm trees and natural undergrowth, where the sound of the lapping waters on the beach is replaced by the wind gently moving through the fronds. Along its northern and eastern shores the island's beach is a narrow strip of sand, while, at its extremities, large sand banks form according to the prevailing current which moves the sand from east to west during the six months between November and April, and back again to the eastern side during the remaining six months. This is characteristic of many of the Maldivian islands that lie near channels.

At Vilamendhoo sewerage is stored in tanks, treated and used to fertilize the island. No waste pollutes the wonderful **house reef** that, from close to the shore, drops down to 20m (66ft) and more. The reef has five marked entry and exit points for snorkellers and scuba divers. The prevailing current gives divers a ride on a pleasant drift dive. It is this same current that, during the months of October and November, brings in the abundant plankton that attracts manta rays and whale sharks.

The size of the resort is 900m (2952ft) long and 300m (984ft) wide and it has 141 simple rooms with air conditioning. Some of the excursions arranged include shopping in Malé, aerial photoflips and fishing trips.

Rasdhoo Atoll Resort Islands
Kuramathi ★★

This is a long, wide island 55km (34 miles) west of Hulhule, on the southern rim of the small Rasdhoo Atoll. Transfer from the airport is one hour and 40 minutes by air-conditioned speedboat or 20 minutes flying. A shuttle bus service covering 1.5km (1 mile) connects the three hotel resorts of the island. There are a total of 274 bungalows, water villas and suites, most with air conditioning, hot and cold water and some with a fridge. With lots of restaurants, bars, shops and a disco, this is an island for fun-seekers and those who enjoy a variety of venues. Apart from the standard facilities there are also tennis courts and sunset cruises.

Kuramathi is surrounded by a great **house reef**. The more interesting area for the snorkeller is on the inside of the atoll where the waters are calmer and corals have not been damaged by the pounding current that flows past the southern side. Until 1970 Kuramathi was inhabited by a local fishing community which was subsequently moved to a nearby island when the resorts became operational.

Veligandu ★★

A medium-range resort situated on the northern rim of Rasdhoo, Veligandu lies some 57km (35 miles) west of Hulhule. The speedboat transfer takes about one hour and 40 minutes, but it's only 20 minutes by air.

The 73 rooms all have a sea view and are equipped with air conditioning, hot and cold fresh water, a mini bar and telephone. This is a small island with lovely beaches and a wide sand bank, perfect for lazing in the sun, while the energetic can indulge in the usual water sports, volleyball and table tennis.

KURAMATHI'S THREE VILLAGES
Kuramathi's length seemed appropriate for the development of **three hotel resorts**, each different in style and character. **Kuramathi Village** is the largest on the island and boasts 90 terraced apartments with air conditioning and 34 modest, thatched bungalows. It has a spacious restaurant with a sun deck and a wooden jetty, a bar set behind an old wooden *dhoni* and covered by a steep, thatched roof. Further along the long, sandy beach, **Cottage Club** offers 80 bungalows for the more reserved guest looking for tranquillity and solitude. At the thin end of the island **Blue Lagoon Club** has 30 conventional rooms and 20 wooden water villas. Spilling over onto the water's edge is the wooden deck of the bar where guests gather at sunset to witness the feeding of the stingrays by staff members.

FELIDHU (VAAVU) ATOLL

Felidhu also includes Vattaru Atoll. The local inhabitants of the atoll are mainly fisherfolk. Early in the morning fishing boats leave the protected harbours of their villages to search the seas for fishing grounds. The two resorts on the atoll are both situated on its northeastern outer rim.

Alimatha Aquatic Resort **

This is a medium-range resort 58km (36 miles) south of the airport on the rim of Felidhu Atoll, and it's 120 minutes by speedboat to get there. It takes about 15 minutes to walk around the island and there are 96 beach bungalows and six water bungalows built on stilts. All rooms have a terrace and air conditioning, ceiling fan, hot and cold water, mini bar and safe box. The island was recently redeveloped, is managed by an Italian company and has a strong Italian flavour and clientele!

Good snorkelling is found a fair distance from the beach, otherwise a boat takes snorkellers out every day. Sailing, windsurfing, night fishing, island-hopping, scuba diving, and deep-sea fishing are offered. The island is heavily vegetated and is reputed to have the tallest coconut palms in the atoll.

Felidhu Atoll

Dhiggiri **

This small resort island is situated on the northern rim of Felidhu Atoll; its distance from the airport is 48km (30 miles). It takes about an hour and a half by speedboat to arrive at the resort.

Dhiggiri has 45 air-conditioned rooms; these include 10 water villas. Good house reef.

Ari and Felidhu Atolls at a Glance

BEST TIMES TO VISIT

The balmiest, lovliest days are between November and April. A gentle breeze cools the days and nights but brings no clouds. December and January are particularly hot while the wet months occur here from May to October.

GETTING THERE

Charter flights and national airlines from many international destinations have regular flights that land at **Hulhule**, Maldives' International Airport.

GETTING AROUND

It is not advisable to transfer to an island resort on **Ari** or **Felidhu Atoll** aboard a motorized *dhoni* as the journey will be too long. Most resort islands transfer their guests aboard a speedboat – the larger ones have air-conditioned interiors. Crossing channels between Malé and the atolls can be bumpy and for those who suffer from motion sickness, flying is the alternative. Seaplanes reach almost all corners of Ari. Only seaplanes visit Felidhu Atoll. For charter companies at Hulhule see Travel Tips.

WHERE TO STAY

Ari Atoll
Angaga Tourist Resort, tel: 45-0510, fax: 45-0520; Malé, tel: 31-3523, fax: 31-3522.
Athuruga, tel: 45-0508, fax: 45-0574; Malé, tel: 31-0489, fax: 31-0390.
Bathala Island Resort, tel: 45-0587, fax: 45-0558; Malé, tel: 31-5236, fax: 31-5237.
Dhoni Mighili, tel: 45-0751, fax: 45-0727; Malé, tel: 33-2287, fax: 31-4875.
Ellaidhoo Tourist Resort, tel: 45-0586, fax: 45-0514; Malé, tel: 31-7717, fax: 31-4977.
Fesdu Fun Island (Fesdhoo), tel: 45-0541, fax: 45-0547; Malé, tel: 32-3080, fax: 32-2678.
Gangehi Club, tel: 45-0505, fax: 45-0506; Malé, tel: 31-3937, fax: 31-3939.
Halaveli Holiday Island, tel: 45-0559, fax: 45-0564; Malé, tel: 32-2719, fax: 32-3463.
Hilton Maldives, tel: 45-0629, fax: 45-0619; Malé, tel: 32-2432, fax: 32-4009.
Holiday Island, tel: 45-0011, fax: 45-0022; Malé, tel: 31-6161, fax: 31-4565.
Kuda Rah Island Resort, tel: 45-0610, fax: 45-0550; Malé, tel: 31-3937, fax: 31-3939.
Lily Beach, tel: 45-0013, fax: 45-0646; Malé, tel: 31-7464, fax: 31-7466.
Maayaafushi, tel: 45-0588, fax: 45-0568; Malé, tel: 32-3524, fax: 32-2516.
Machchafushi, tel: 45-4545, fax: 45-4546; Malé , tel: 31-7080, fax: 31-8014.
Madoogali, tel: 45-0581, fax: 45-0554; Malé, tel: 31-7975, fax: 31-7974.
Mirihi, tel: 45-0500, fax: 45-0501; Malé, tel/fax: 32-5448.
Moofushi, tel: 45-0598, fax: 45-0509; Malé, tel: 32-6141, fax: 31-3237.
Nika Hotel, tel: 45-0516, fax: 45-0577; Malé, tel: 31-4541, fax: 32-5097.
Ranveli Village, tel: 45-0570, fax: 45-0523; Malé, tel: 31-6921, fax: 31-6922.
Sun Island Resort, tel: 45-0088, fax: 45-0099; Malé, tel: 31-6161, fax: 31-4565.
Thudufushi, tel: 45-0597, fax: 45-0515; Malé, tel: 31-0489, fax: 31-0390.
Twin Island (Maafushivaru), tel: 45-0596, fax: 45-0524; Malé, tel: 32-3080, fax: 32-0274.
Vakarufali, tel: 45-0004, fax: 45-007; Malé office, tel: 31-4149, fax: 31-4150.
Velidhoo, tel: 45-0551, fax: 45-0630; Malé, tel: 31-3738, fax: 32-6264.
Vilamendhoo, tel: 45-0637, fax: 45-0639; Malé, tel: 31-6131, fax: 32-4943.
White Sands Resort (Dhidhdhoofinolhu), tel: 45-0513, fax: 45-0512; Malé, tel: 32-1930, fax: 32-7355.

Rasdhoo Atoll
Kuramathi Tourist Resort, tel: 45-0527, fax: 45-0556; Malé, tel: 32-3080, fax: 32-0274.
Veligandu, tel: 45-0519, fax: 45-0648; Malé, tel: 32-2432, fax: 32-4009.

Felidhu Atoll
Alimatha, tel: 45-0575, fax: 45-0544; Malé, tel: 32-3524, fax: 32-2516.
Dhiggiri, tel: 45-0593, fax: 45-0592; Malé, tel: 32-3524, fax: 32-2516.

8
Under Maldivian Waters

Like a floating iceberg with its bulk submerged, so too does most of Maldives occur underwater. Small and flat, the islands of Maldives have a limited variety of flora and fauna when compared to the infinite abundance of marine life found on their coral reefs. **Soft** and **hard corals**, **tiny shrimps**, **turtles**, **manta rays**, **sharks**, **reef fish**, **moray eels**, **shells** and **sea slugs** are only a few of the immense variety of species that inhabit one of the greatest reef systems in the world. Ninety per cent of visitors to Maldives spend most of their time with their heads submerged in the crystalline waters, marvelling at the natural aquarium that has made this archipelago so famous.

Corals do not grow if the water temperature is below 20°C (68°F), and with an average water temperature of **28°C (82°F)**, the ocean surrounding Maldives is ideal for thriving coral growth.

In enclosed sea areas such as the Red Sea and many bays, the salinity level of the water may rise too high, having an adverse effect on coral communities. Similarly, low salinity levels also affect coral growth – where a river meets the sea and in areas where extensive rainfall alters the salinity level of the surface waters. Fortunately, the Maldivian reef system lies in mid-ocean and has **no rivers**, and the weather pattern never reaches cyclonic proportions. There is also an absence of sedimentation and an abundance of nutrients which creates a perfect environment for Maldivian reefs, a natural wonder that has taken millions of years to develop into the diverse and thriving world that one can admire today.

INDIA

Laccadive Islands

SRI LANKA

• Malé   INDIAN OCEAN
Maldives

Equator

DON'T MISS

*** A snorkelling safari: a daily excursion from your resort island to a reef.
*** A diving trip to a manta point: diving with these majestic creatures is a highlight for most people.
** Spotting giant clams: they often have their shells ajar.
* Flying fish: when riding in a *dhoni*, keep a lookout for startled flying fish.

Opposite: *Many resort islands are surrounded by a shallow house reef perfect for snorkelling and diving.*

Sea Life
Corals

Hard (*Scleractinia*) and **soft corals** (*Alcyonacea*) belong to the group called **Cnidaria** (previously known as Coelenterata), which includes jellyfish, gorgonians (sea fans) and sea anemones. Hard corals are often mistaken for rocks and are generally found in the shallower waters up to a depth of 50m (164ft), at which sunlight penetrates clear water. Coral has many small holes that pock the hard structure. At night, the coral polyps extend tentacles out of these holes to feed on the microscopic animals suspended in the water. The tentacles are armed with poisonous cells used to catch prey. Other cells produce a slimy substance which protects the polyp, and as dust and sand slide over this slimy surface food is captured and foreign materials removed.

Soft corals are often mistaken for plants because of their flowery structures. Unlike hard corals, they do not host algae and therefore do not need to limit their existence to the well-lit areas on the reef. They are to be found at all depths and abound in caves and under overhangs.

All **Cnidaria** have stinging cells in their tentacles which they use to defend themselves. In some species the stinging cells are weak and if touched by humans will cause little irritation. On the other hand, stinging cells of the Hydrozoa class of corals can be painful. **Fire corals** (*Millepora*) belong to this class and deliver a nasty sting when touched. Once identified, their yellow-brown hard structures are easily distinguishable from other corals.

THE REEF BUILDERS

In simple terms, it can be said that the formation of a coral reef is the build-up of **hard corals**, generation after generation. Most hard corals form colonies of **coral polyps** (each an individual creature that catches and digests its own food) that produce a hard, **limestone skeleton**. When the polyps die they decompose, leaving a relatively indestructible white, calcium skeleton. **Pink coralline algae** grows over the pieces of coral skeleton, cementing them into a concrete whole and new coral colonies grow over the dead coral, gradually building up the reef.

Crustaceans (*Arthropods*)

These nocturnal reef dwellers are seldom seen during the day as they hide in small crevices and under overhangs. In Maldives the most common **crustaceans** are **shrimps**, **crabs** and **lobsters**. Fortunately, Maldivians have never acquired a taste for lobster and have only recently started catching this crustacean for the tourist's dinner plate.

Most crabs (*Brachyura*) have a thick, hard shield but the **hermit crab** (*Anomura*) twists its body into a mollusc's shell. When his adopted home becomes too small, he abandons it for a bigger one. **Ghost crabs** (*Ocypode*) are nocturnal predators that live in small burrows on the sandy beaches of most islands. The **rock crab** (*Grapsus*) is a dark green and black crab that is perfectly camouflaged against the wet and slimy rocks of a jetty. Not seen on the resort islands, the **land crab** (*Goecarcinus*) has been sighted in the mangrove swamps of the far northern islands, while the **porcelain crab** with its oversized pincer, is not common.

Molluscs (*Mollusca*)

There are three different groups of molluscs inhabiting Maldivian reefs: **sea snails** and **sea slugs** (*Gastropoda*), **clams** and **mussels** (*Bivalvia*) and **octopus**, **squid** and **cuttlefish** (*Cephalopoda*).

Unfortunately the shells found on shop shelves are not the empty encasings of **gastropods** found on the beach. These are usually picked live from the reefs, killed, dried and polished before finding their way into display cabinets. As a result, a few shell species like the **conch** and **trident shells** have become extremely rare. **Cowries** abound on the beaches but collecting shells is illegal.

Opposite: *Featherstars sway gently in the current collecting tiny organisms suspended in the water.* **Below:** *Giant clams lie on the reef with open shells.*

Sea slugs (*Opisthobranchia*) are animals without shells. Many are poisonous or have bad tasting cells within their body structure, while others incorporate stinging cells in their tissue. **Clams** and **mussels** (*Bivalvia*) often find their way onto a dining table as palatable delicacies from the sea. **Giant clams** (*Tridacna*) with strong muscles are common on Maldivian reefs.

You should consider yourself very fortunate if you do catch a glimpse of **octopus**, **squid** or **cuttlefish** (*Cephalopods*) in Maldives as these creatures are not often seen. Squid live in schools while the octopus and the cuttlefish are found alone on the reef.

The **starfish** (*Echinoderms*) is easily recognizable in its five-sided, or pentagonal, symmetry. There are five main groups in this phylum (or group) of marine invertebrates, all common in Maldivian waters. The **Crown-of-thorns** (*Acanthaster planci*) is the only one, though, that threatens the reefs. It is a multiple-armed, bulky starfish that is covered in venomous spines. It is the most voracious coral predator of the world's coral reefs, destroying entire reefs when a group of these starfish congregate to feed. Maldivian reefs have been affected by this ruthless marine creature only in small isolated patches.

In some cases management encouraged scuba divers to collect the pests, but as quickly as the starfish were removed, they were replaced. This periodic increase is probably nature's own way of maintaining a varied coral species, eliminating the abundant, faster-growing ones.

The Fish of Maldives

The Maldivian islands occur almost at the centre of the seasonal ebb and flow of monsoon-driven currents, making them a lively showcase for an extensive array of fish numbering in excess of 1000 species. A plastic fish chart is useful on a snorkelling or diving outing.

Of the various species that graze over the reef, a favourite of snorkellers and scuba divers is the **powderblue surgeonfish** (*Acanthurus leucosternon*) which is often found in the shallows, swimming in tightly-packed schools that are easy to photograph. The oval and compressed body is bright blue in colour, it has a black face and a white band connecting the chin to the pectoral fin. The dorsal fin is yellow and so are the two 'scalpels' at the base of its tail. It attains a maximum length of 20cm (8 in).

Another fish that is common on outer reef slopes and in areas of rich coral growth is the **emperor angelfish** (*Pomacanthus imperator*). It is easily identifiable by the alternating yellow and blue stripes that line the body horizontally. Its eyes are masked by a thick black stripe lined with blue, its mouth is white. Look closely in sheltered areas of the reef, under ledges and in caves for the juvenile which, very different to the adult, is dark blue and has white concentric circles adorning its body. **Butterflyfish** (*Chaetodontidae*) are small, disc-like and colourful fish found in pairs among the corals or in schools, hovering in a gentle current. Most butterflyfish have a dark line stretching over the eye and some

MONEY COWRIES

So important was this little **cowrie** (*Cyprea moneta*) to ancient trade that even its Latin name expresses its monetary usage. The shell abounds in the tropics of the **Indo-Pacific Ocean**, but it was the Maldivians who devised a way of collecting cowries that made the islands the centre of trade. The locals placed palm leaves in the shallows and cowries were attracted to the detritus that had accumulated on the fronds. The laden leaves were pulled onto the beach where the cowries were left to die and fall off the leaves. The shells were buried in the sand so that the animals decomposed, leaving only shiny shells. Cowrie shells have been found in Norway, Thailand and Bengal and in the 14th century Ibn Battutah found evidence of cowrie shells in West Africa. Today their historical monetary importance has not been forgotten: a drawing of the cowrie appears on **Maldivian bank notes**.

Left: *The red-tailed butterflyfish is a common inhabitor of Maldivian reefs. Schools float above coral heads making for perfect photographic opportunities.* **Opposite:** *Octopus, which are not easily seen, are usually found alone on the reef.*

DOLPHINS

Often, while on transfer to your resort island or on a slow-moving *dhoni* during an excursion, playful schools of **bottlenose dolphins** (*Tursiops truncatus*) will dance in the frothy wake of the boat. Sometimes their high-pitched sounds may be heard while diving or snorkelling, but it is unlikely that you will be able to dive or swim with them as they are shy mammals and wary of humans in the water. **Spinner dolphins** (*Stenella longirostris*) reach a maximum length of about 1.8m (6ft). As a boat approaches a school, they go into a 'playing frenzy', churning the water and hurling themselves high into the air, giving the onlookers an exciting show.

have a dark spot near their tails. This seemingly ornamental pattern is actually a carefully developed design to confuse a predator into thinking that the fish is actually facing the opposite way and, as it starts to chase it, the butterflyfish darts off in the opposite direction.

Batfish (*Ephippidae*) are beautiful longfin fish well known to divers. They float in mid-water over reefs and play with divers' bubbles. Juveniles are found in shallow lagoons and near jetties where they float motionlessly, resembling submerged dead leaves.

Snappers (*Lutjanidae*) are found in Maldives, the most common being the **bluestriped snapper** (*Lutjanus kasmira*) and **humphead snapper** (*Lutjanus gibbus*). They are found in large schools hovering in the current over well-formed reefs.

Moray eels (*Muraenidae*) are long and snake-like with sharp, inward-pointing teeth. They hunt for small fish at night and during the day they are found in holes which they choose according to their body size and which they may occupy for years. Morays are not aggressive creatures but can deliver a nasty bite if provoked.

Pelagic Fish

Pelagic fish live in the open sea. They visit the reef only to feed, preferring the subdued lighting of dusk and dawn or the darker hours of the night. Part of the group of pelagic fish found in Maldives are: **barracudas** (*Sphyraenida*), **jacks** or **trevallies** (*Carangidae*), **tunas** and **mackerels** (*Scombridae*) and some **sharks**. Most sharks are harmless; in fact, most shark species are quite small, measuring less than 2m (6.5ft) in length. Many are deep-water species never seen near coral reefs where divers tend to venture; and certainly in Maldives with its abundance of fishes, sharks are not known to have attacked humans. While diving on a reef it is almost certain that you will encounter a shark or two, and you will notice that they are shy, preferring to move away rather than going towards a bubbling, noisy scuba diver.

Grey reef sharks (*Carcharhinus amblyrhynchos*) patrol the outer reefs while small **whitetip reef sharks** (*Triaenodon obesus*) are often seen resting on the reef, darting away quickly if a diver ventures too close. Many Maldivian islands have a resident, harmless, baby **blacktip reef shark** (*Carcharhinus melanopterus*) swimming in their shallows. Even snorkellers will have the exciting pleasure of sighting at least one of the three species of reef sharks common in these waters.

With a small dose of luck, scuba divers may have the added pleasure of encountering the **scalloped hammerhead**, the **nurse shark**, the **leopard shark** and the **whale shark**. The nurse shark (*Nebrius ferrugineus*) is known as *nidhan miyaru* or 'sleeping shark' in Dhivehi. It is a bottom dweller, found resting in caves and under overhangs during the day. The whale shark (*Rhincodon typus*), the largest fish in the world, seasonally visits Maldives when plankton is abundant and occasionally one is spotted by a boatload of fortunate divers. Other sharks present in Maldivian territory that prefer the deeper waters are almost never seen near the reefs.

Rays

In Maldives the **bluespotted stingray** (*Taeniura lymma*) lives on the reefs and hides under overhangs. The **blackspotted ribbontail stingray** (*Taeniura meyeni*) is normally found in channels or on sandy patches near the reef and the **spotted eagle ray** (*Aetobatus narinari*) is often seen 'flying' past a reef or in the shallow lagoons.

DANGEROUS FISH

The **stonefish** (*Synanceia verrucosa*) is the ugliest fish on the reef. Due to its sedentary and camouflaged habit, it is probably the most dangerous of the sea creatures – the **scorpionfish** (*Scorpaenidae)* belongs to the same family. Lying on the reef like a harmless rock, the stonefish waits for a fish to swim nearby and with lightning speed, it sucks in its prey. Vulnerable to predators, it has developed a defence mechanism equipped with a powerful venom:

13 poisonous spines line its back and, when touched, inject venom into the victim. The pain inflicted is excruciating, the venom causes shock and temporary paralysis and even death. Hot water, at 50°C (122°F), will relieve the pain and break down the protein venom. The wound should not be immobilized or constricted by a bandage. Movement of the limb will cause the dispersion of the venom and its dilution. See a doctor immediately; anti-venom is available.

Divers get excited at the sight of a shark, a rare fish or an eagle ray, but no other fish is able to stimulate such elated emotions as the **manta ray** (*Manta birostris*). Mantas approach a reef only when they need to be cleaned, and hover motionlessly over a piece of coral as tiny **cleaner wrasse** eat parasites off their skin. There are many cleaning stations in Maldives that are visited regularly by mantas. Another chance to enjoy the company of the mantas is when they come in to feed when plankton blooms (May to November).

Above: *A manta ray glides into the deep blue.*
Below: *Turtles are often seen in Maldivian waters and since 1995 they have been a protected species.*

Turtles

Two species of turtles are common in Maldivian waters; the **hawksbill** (*Eretmochelys imbricata*) and the **green turtle** (*Chelonia mydas*), while the **loggerhead** (*Caretta caretta*), the **leatherback** (*Dermochelys coriacea*) and the **Olive Ridley** (*Lepidochelys olivacea*) are rare visitors of these waters.

The sight of a turtle is exciting to divers but they do not realize the damage they can cause when they touch it and keep it underwater for too long. Turtles breathe air and when sleeping, their metabolism slows down, allowing them to stay underwater for over an hour. If suddenly awakened, they need to surface for a fresh gulp of air. If a diver holds on to one, it may drown.

HARMFUL STINGRAYS

Stingrays have the habit of burying themselves in the sand and if they feel threatened, they lash out at the intruder with their whip-like tails, equipped with venomous, barbed spines. These cause serious wounds and if you are stung by a stingray, you should wash the wound immediately with sea water and remove any spines that may have broken off. Immerse the wound in water of about 50°C (122°F) or as hot as you can take it, without burning the area. Hot water can relieve the pain and break down the protein venom. See a doctor as soon as possible.

SNORKELLING AND SCUBA DIVING

Whether you are an experienced scuba diver, a beginner or a first-timer, Maldivian reefs provide the perfect niche for your level of experience. If you have not yet discovered the underwater world, this is the place to don mask, fins and snorkel and embark on a journey through one of the **richest marine ecosystems** on earth. For first-time snorkellers and scuba divers, Maldivian reefs offer the perfect learning ground as the water surrounding the islands is calm, clear and warm and marine life abounds.

Snorkellers can hire equipment from the resort island's water-sport centre, however it is advisable to bring your own mask, fins and snorkel as it is more comfortable to use equipment with which you are already familiar.

Before embarking on your snorkelling adventure ask at the water-sport centre for advice on where to go; and if you are unsure on how to snorkel or how to use your equipment ask a staff member to give you a quick course. Most diving schools on the islands accept all well-known qualifications: **PADI, NAUI, CMAS, BSAC** and **SSI**. Dive schools have equipment for hire, from masks, snorkels and fins to dive computers, torches and underwater cameras and housings. Dives on a house reef may be done throughout the day, as long as you dive with a buddy. Most resort islands offer two boat trips a day to surrounding reefs and a night dive. Diving safaris are organized to remote areas of the atolls.

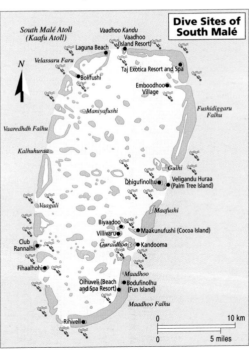

Dive Sites of South Malé

South Malé Atoll (Kaafu Atoll)
Vaadhoo Kandu
Vaadhoo (Island Resort)
Laguna Beach
Velassaru Faru
N
Bolifushi
Taj Exotica Resort and Spa
Emboodhoo Village
Maniyafushi
Fushidiggaru Falhu
Vaaredhdh Falhu
Kalhuhuraa
Gulhi
Dhigufinolhu
Veligandu Huraa (Palm Tree Island)
Vaagali
Maafushi
Biyaadoo
Villivaru
Maakunufushi (Cocoa Island)
Club Rannalhi
Guraidhoo
Kandooma
Fihaalhohi
Maadhoo
Olhuveli (Beach and Spa Resort)
Bodufinolhu (Fun Island)
Maadhoo Falhu
Rihiveli

0   10 km
0   5 miles

Above: *Beautiful reefs that surround the islands plunge to the bottom of the ocean.*

KURAMATHI HOUSE REEF

Kuramathi is a resort island situated on the southern rim of the **Rasdhoo Atoll**. Its shallow house reef offers great snorkelling opportunities. You will see a variety of marine life: from schools of **squid** to free-swimming **moray eels, bluespotted stingrays** and **reef fishes**. The deeper house reef offers a comfortable dive among large coral heads and their inhabitants. A recent, small wreck lies on the sand which is becoming encrusted with **corals, sponges** and other marine organisms. Morays are known to choose a lair and keep it as their home for a long time, so perhaps, when you visit this site you will still see Emma, the giant moray eel, that presides over the coral outcrops.

Popular Dive Sites

There is something unexplainable about plunging into the depths while breathing through a mechanical apparatus, floating over the edge but never falling, listening to the sounds of a living reef. The coral polyps of Maldives have developed an enormous and very complex structure that, today, is the playground of sport divers. The dive sites of Maldives are innumerable. As new resorts are opened, new sites are discovered, and as it becomes easier to explore the further reaches of the atolls, diving possibilities are becoming endless. There are too many beautiful and unique dive spots to mention in this chapter but those included below are favourite sites.

Madivaru Kandu: situated on the southern rim of the small **Rasdhoo Atoll**, northeast of the **Ari (Alifu) Atoll**, Madivaru Kandu is a great wall dive. However, early in the morning, as dawn breaks, divers swim away from the wall and towards the big blue and wait. At a maximum depth of 30m (100ft) the migration of the hammerhead sharks can be witnessed. Slow-moving and very shy, these sharks seldom come close to divers. Madivaru Kandu is probably the best known site in Maldives for hammerheads. Nobody has yet understood the reason for their daily appearance here, or why they come to this relatively shallow depth.

Halaveli wreck: on the northeastern side of the **Ari (Alifu) Atoll**, along the same reef that holds the resort island of Halaveli, a wreck was purposely sunk in 1991 and lies on a sand bed at 28m (92ft). **Blackspotted stingrays** often come to greet divers and playfully circle them with their disc-like bodies.

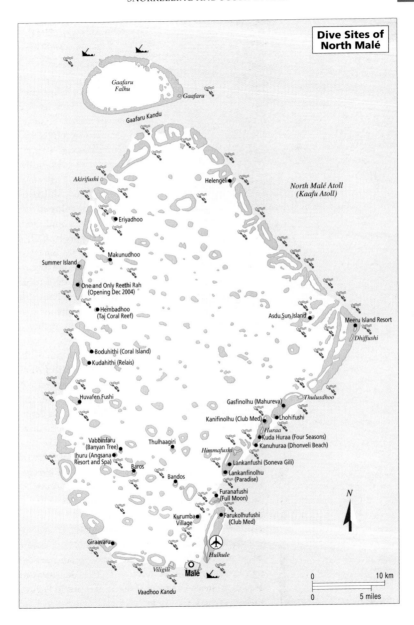

Dive Sites of North Malé

Gaafaru Falhu

Gaafaru

Gaafaru Kandu

Akirifushi

Helengeli

North Malé Atoll (Kaafu Atoll)

Eriyadhoo

Makunudhoo

Summer Island

One and Only Reethi Rah (Opening Dec 2004)

Hembadhoo (Taj Coral Reef)

Asdu Sun Island

Meeru Island Resort

Dhiffushi

Boduhithi (Coral Island)

Kudahithi (Relais)

Huvafen Fushi

Gasfinolhu (Mahureva)

Thulusdhoo

Kanifinolhu (Club Med)

Lhohifushi

Huraa

Vabbinfaru (Banyan Tree)

Thulhaagiri

Kuda Huraa (Four Seasons)

Kanuhuraa (Dhonveli Beach)

Ihuru (Angsana Resort and Spa)

Himmafushi

Baros

Lankanfushi (Soneva Gili)

Bandos

Lankanfinolhu (Paradise)

Furanafushi (Full Moon)

Kurumba Village

Farukolhufushi (Club Med)

Giraavaru

Hulhule

N

Viligili

Malé

Vaadhoo Kandu

0   10 km

0   5 miles

Right: Anemones and their resident clownfish provide an amusing show for divers.

Opposite: The Maldive Victory *struck the encircling reef of the Airport Island. Lying on a sandy seabed it is now a popular dive spot.*

Kudarah Tila: lying in the channel between the two islands of **Dhangethi** and **Dhigurah**, on the southern rim of the **Ari Atoll**, Kudarah Tila is probably the best in Maldives, but only for very experienced divers as the currents are very strong. The tila is small and can easily be encircled several times during the dive, enabling you to peruse each part of it. It is covered with a profusion of soft corals of every colour and there is usually an enormous school of bluebanded snappers. Batfish, butterflyfish, sweetlips, clownfish and groupers are also some of the resident inhabitants.

The Ship Yard: on the western rim of the **Lhaviyani Atoll**, near the island of **Felivaru**, divers are given the opportunity to dive two shipwrecks in one dive. The first one, with its rusting bow easily seen above the water, sank during a storm in 1980. The second wreck which lies on the seabed at 30m (100ft), was intentionally sunk by the owners a few months later. Swept by rich currents, these sunken vessels have become footholds for large colourful soft corals while encrusting algae and sponges fight for space along the rusting hulk. With such a rich food source covering the wreck, reef fish swarm the site, which in turn entices the pelagic fish.

Kuredu Express: east of the resort island of **Kuredu** (Kuredhoo) in **Lhavinyani Atoll**, grey reef sharks are regular visitors of this outer reef slope, as are large schools of jacks. Divers descend in the current to the sparsely covered plateau to watch the display unfold.

DIVING AND SNORKELLING

- Don't go into the water alone. It's more fun sharing the experience with someone else and should problems arise, it is best to have the assistance of a dive buddy.
- Protect yourself from the sun. Snorkellers should wear a T-shirt and cotton leggings or Lycra pants as backs and legs can be badly burnt while exposed to the sun. Use sunscreen liberally.
- Don't walk or stand on the reef as you crush living corals. If you get tired or have a problem with your gear, turn on your back, relax and float.
- Don't touch or pick up anything as you may damage it. It's also for your own safety as you may be stung by fire coral or poisoned by a stonefish.
- Don't tire yourself; go slowly and you will see a lot more of the marine life.

Maldive Victory: this wreck sank after striking the reef on the southern tip of Hulhule, the airport island, at a depth of 35m (110ft). The currents are usually strong, but once the divers reach the deck and its open holds, the bulk of the ship can be used as a shield.

HP Reef: this tila is on the eastern side of the southern rim of **North Malé Atoll**. The magnificent explosion of colour created by the soft corals has led a few dive schools to call this area **Rainbow Reef**.

Guraidhoo Channel: on the eastern rim of South Malé Atoll, the long encircling reef of **Maadhoo Falhu** ends, at its northern tip, in the **Guraidhoo Channel**. The drift dive starts along the outside wall and moves towards the corner and into the channel.

Biyaadoo House Reef: surrounding the resort island of Biyaadoo, this must be the most spectacular of Maldivian house reefs. It offers six very different diving possibilities, from drift dives over a bed of fire corals – home to a myriad **reef fish**, **turtles** and visited by reef sharks and eagle rays – to slower-moving dives along a protected wall covered in delicate corals. A huge school of jacks is often seen.

Miyaru Kandu: north of **Alimatha** resort island, this channel cuts through the outer reef on the eastern side of **Felidhu (Vaavu) Atoll**. As you drift along the gently sloping outer wall, look towards the open sea for grey reef sharks and eagle rays. Closer to the reef, small whitetip sharks keep their distance from divers. As you turn into the channel, the reef is enriched with soft and hard corals, hedges of sea fans stand perpendicular to the current and, nestled among the corals, bright, red anemones retract their tentacles.

MARINE FOOD CHAIN

The organisms that make up plankton are plants (*phytoplankton*) such as algae, and animals (*zooplankton*) such as protozoans, crustaceans, jellyfish and the larvae of many invertebrates and fish. Floating with the wind and the tides just under the surface of the water, plankton is a very important part of the marine food chain, being the preferred food source of a variety of animals including filter feeders, small fish, mantas and the largest fish on earth – the whale shark. Plankton blooms from May to November.

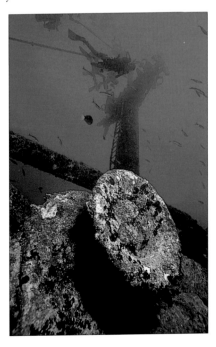

Worldwide It is quite common for islanders who depend on the pickings of the sea for food, to find turtle eggs and turtle flesh a rare delicacy and Maldivian inhabitants are no different. Through time they have collected turtle eggs and killed turtles to supplement their diet with extra protein. Aggravated by the demand from tourists for turtle shell souvenirs, the Maldivian turtle population has diminished.

It is only recently that the government has taken serious steps to stop the unnecessary slaughter by **banning** the **capture** and **killing** of turtles and the **collection** of their **eggs**. Projects have been initiated on certain islands, where young turtles are caught before they reach the water and kept in safety until they are about two years old. They are then tagged and released and, hopefully, are not as vulnerable to predators. The turtles of Maldives were protected in 1995.

ECOLOGICAL AWARENESS

For centuries the villagers survived on homegrown vegetables, coconuts and fishing. Their houses and village buildings were made of coconut thatch or coral rock which they collected from the endless supply of the surrounding reef. What little refuse they produced was thrown out to sea to be taken away by the currents (most of it being biodegradable anyway).

Then the modern world caught up with Maldivians. Little houses of the capital city have become high-rise buildings, coral reefs are being depleted and destroyed. Imported foodstuffs and luxuries packaged in sophisticated plastics and tins are polluting the sea. Tourists have plundered the reefs, removing shells and corals, and bought turtle shell mementos from the locals.

The Maldivian Archipelago is not indestructible. The reefs are extremely sensitive to changes and pollution and Maldivians are taking steps to protect their environment. **Spearfishing** is not allowed and **shell** and **coral collecting** has been banned. **Turtles** are also **protected**.

As a tourist and visitor to the islands you can contribute towards safeguarding this fragile environment. Take nothing from the water and leave nothing behind but your

bubbles. Waste disposal is closely monitored. German tour operators have been giving their clients large plastic bags in which to put non-biodegradable rubbish, accumulated during their stay on the islands. These are then taken back to Germany. Hopefully, in the near future, before it is too late, everyone will follow their good example.

Right: *Soft corals adorn reef slopes. These tree-like animals extend their tentacles into the current to feed.*

Maldivian Waters at a Glance

The **water temperatures** vary from 26°C (79°F) during the rainy season between May and October to 30°C (86°F) during the dry months between February and April. In the shallow lagoons the water temperature rarely drops below 32°C (90°F). The dry northeast monsoon prevails from December to March and visibility reaches 40m (131ft) in this period. As the monsoon winds change to southwesterly in May, plankton blooms and visibility can be reduced to about 20m (65ft). Choppy seas occur during the windier months of the rainy period – June and October. And, as the calmest seas and bluest skies occur between the months of November and May, the best time of the year for a perfect diving holiday is during **March** and **April**. To watch the spectacle of feeding mantas, be prepared to sacrifice visibility as plankton particles are rich in the waters. Plankton blooms occur mainly during the wet monsoon from May to November.

SNORKELLING

Resorts have equipment for hire but it is advisable to bring your own mask, fins and snorkel as you will be more comfortable with your own equipment. This way it is also less expensive!

DIVING

All dive schools have equipment for hire, but it is advisable to bring your own set as you would be more familiar with it. You should not need a wetsuit thicker than 3mm; during the warmer months, a Lycra suit is sufficient. If you intend doing multiple dives it would be advisable to bring a computer. A cylinder and weight belt are supplied by the dive schools and are automatically included in the price of the dive. Bring proof of your diving qualification. All diving schools are strict on safety.

Decompression sickness: this can happen any time between your climbing onto the boat to 24 hours after diving. Itchy skin, pain in the joints, ringing of the ears, nausea, fatigue, faintness, loss of balance, unconsciousness and paralysis are symptoms.

SAFETY MEASURES

● Diligently follow your dive tables or computer.
● Don't dive deeper than 30m (100ft) – a Maldivian law.
● Don't go into decompression but do a safety stop at 5m (16ft).
● Don't dive if you feel tired or if you overindulged the night before.
● Don't dive after you've done strenuous physical exercise and don't do any strenuous physical exercise after a dive.
● Double your normal intake of liquids, preferably drink

fruit juices and drinks that include electrolytes. Cut down on caffeine and alcohol intake.
● No flying for at least 12 hours after your last dive.
● For any diving emergency contact: **Bandos Medical and Hyperbaric Treatment Centre**. Bandos Island Resort, tel: 44-0088, fax: 44-0060.

LEARN TO SCUBA DIVE

It is advisable to do a diving course before you come to Maldives, so you can start diving immediately, instead of spending almost a week of your holiday in the classroom. Most resorts have a diving school with qualified, professional diving instructors. If you do opt to do a diving course during your stay it is advisable, prior to your departure, to obtain a medical certificate stating that you are of sound health for diving, as not all resorts have a resident doctor staying on the island. You must know how to swim, obviously, and be 12 years of age or older.

DIVE OPERATORS

Most resort islands have a dive school (see contact numbers for resorts and Northern Atolls at a Glance – Tours and Excursions p. 57, for companies that cater for diving safaris). Dive prices include tank and weights but do not usually include the boat ride to the dive site.

Travel Tips

Tourist Information

The Republic of Maldives lies 600km (372 miles) southwest of India and 670km (415 miles) west of Sri Lanka. The archipelago is well-served by international airlines. Boats, speedboats and sea-planes connect the islands while the local airline does trips to the few outlying regional airports.

Maldives Tourism Promotion Board, Aage Building, 3rd Floor, 12 Boduthakurufaanu Magu, Malé, 2004, tel: 32-3228, fax: 32-3229, website:www. visitmaldives.com e-mail: mtpb@visitmaldives.com The Board supplies all the information on Maldives. It also provides assistance or telephone numbers and addresses of resorts that tourists and visitors to the country may require.

Ministry of Home Affairs, Huravee Building, Malé, tel: 32-1752, fax: 32-4739. Open daily 07:30–13:30, closed Fridays. Responsible for censorship of books, videos and films; you will need per-mission from them before you may distribute or sell any material in Maldives.

Addu Development Authority, H. Murmarudhoshuge, Medhuziyaaraiy Magu, Malé, tel: 32-3101, fax: 32-8836. They supply all the informa-tion on Seenu (Addu) Atoll.

Travel Bookings

Hotel and **resort island bookings** should be finalized before arriving in Maldives to ensure a confirmed reservation and a better price. Travel agents as well as various resort booking offices on Malé can also make resort reserva-tions, but direct bookings on Malé are not advisable, as travel agents abroad secure competitive block bookings to specific resorts.

Entry Requirements

All foreigners including Israeli citizens are welcome in Maldives. Visitors need a valid passport to gain entry and are given a 30-day visa on arrival.

Embassies/Consulates: Only a few countries have diplomatic representation in Maldives, each maintaining one office in Malé. These are:

Bangladesh, tel: 31-5541, fax: 31-5543;
Denmark, tel: 31-5175, fax: 32-3523;
France, tel: 31-7255, emergency tel: 77-2784;
Germany, tel: 32-2971;
India, tel: 32-3016, fax: 32-4778;
New Zealand, tel: 32-2432;
Norway, tel: 31-5176, fax: 32-3523;
Pakistan, tel: 32-3005, fax: 31-1823;
Sri Lanka, tel: 32-2845, fax: 32-1652;
Sweden, tel: 32-5174, fax: 32-3523;
UK, tel: 31-1205, fax: 32-5704;
The nearest embassy for USA, France and Germany is at Colombo, Sri Lanka.

Customs

All luggage is opened and searched on arrival by customs officials who check for illegal items that contravene Islamic law. Any alcohol will be removed but you will be given a receipt for it and the bottles will be returned to you on your departure. Pornography is not permitted and most magazines and newspapers are checked page by page and either confiscated, or the revealing pages torn out and the publication returned to you. Cassette tapes have to be viewed by the censorship board. Customs keep the tapes and issue a receipt with which you can collect the tape from the censorship board in Malé after they have checked the video. This process may take a few weeks. As this is a devout Islamic country, dogs, pork, firearms and drugs are also forbidden.

Health Requirements

Visitors from, or passing through, a yellow fever zone must be able to produce a valid International Certificate of Vaccination. Such zones extend through most of tropical Africa and South America (air travellers in airport transit are exempt). Cholera and smallpox certificates are not required, and there is no screening for AIDS. Although malaria was present in Maldives it has been successfully eradicated and there is no need to take anti-malaria precautions.

Getting There

Maldives can only be reached by air, boat and yacht .
By air: Hulhule International Airport, tel: 32-2073/4/5/6, fax: 32-1339, is an island only 4km (2.5 miles) from the capital city, accessible by taxi *dhonis* or speedboats. The regular ferry rides to the island

of Malé take 10 minutes.
Island Aviation, tel: 33-5544, fax: 31-4806, is the local airline and runs regular transfers to the four national airports: Hanimaadhoo on south Thiladhunmathi Atoll, Kah'dhoo on Hadhddunmathi Atoll, Kaadeh'dhoo on north Huvadhu Atoll and Gan on Addu Atoll.
By boat: A few visitors may decide to cross between Sri Lanka and Maldives aboard one of the ships that sail between Colombo and Malé.
By yacht: Yachtsmen wishing to sail around the islands must go through customs in Malé and then apply for a Cruising Permit at the **Ministry of Atolls Administration**, Faashanaa Building, Marine Drive, Malé, tel: 32-3070.

What to Pack

Maldives enjoys a tropical climate. Pack light cotton clothing rather than synthetics. This is a Muslim country so women must cover their shoulders and wear skirts or trousers of below knee-length when visiting a local village or the capital city. Men must wear a shirt and shorts or trousers on such occasions. Dress on the resort islands is generally informal; shorts and T-shirts are the norm all year round (beachwear, though, is appropriate only at the beach, and at the pool). Sunscreen and sunglasses are essential. Swimming and snorkelling gear is a must. You may want to dress 'smart casual' after dark at the up-market resorts.

USEFUL PHRASES

Peace be unto you (Hello) •
As-Salam Alai-kum
How are you? •
haalu kihineh?
Thank you • shuk riyaa
Yes • aah
No • noon
You are welcome •
kale-ah mar-haba
Where? • koba?
When? • kon ira kun?
One • eke
Two • dheiy
How much is this? •
mi kihaa varaka?
Drinking water •
bor feng
To swim • fathahee
To sail • dhunvanee
Atoll • atolu
Island • fushi, rah
Reef • faru
Beach • athiri mathi
Tomorrow • maadhan
Today • miadhu
Where is the boat for . . . ? •
. . . dhoani kobaa?
I do not understand •
ma shakah nuvis-ney

Money Matters

Currency: The Maldivian currency is the Rufiyaa (MRF), divided into 100 Laari (L). Coins are issued in denominations of 1L, 2L, 10L, 25L, 50L, 1MRF and 2MRF; notes are available in denominations of 5MRF, 10MRF, 20MRF, 50MRF, 100MRF and 500MRF. Remember to keep US$10 available to pay the airport tax on your departure.
Banks: Normal banking hours are from 08:30–13:00, Sunday to Thursday. Traveller's cheques may be cashed at any bank and at most hotels.

Credit cards: Most hotels, shops and tour operators accept international credit cards. Arrangements vary from island to island, and it is advisable to check with your credit card company for details of merchant acceptability and other facilities which may be available.

Currency exchange: Foreign money can easily be converted into Rufiyaa in Malé, but it is not necessary at resort islands where hotel payments may be done in major foreign currencies, traveller's cheques or credit cards. Most shops accept US dollars.

Currency restrictons: There are no restrictions on imports or exports. Transactions in resorts and hotels can be made in most hard currencies.

Taxes: There is no VAT.

Tipping: Provided you receive satisfactory service, it is usual to tip porters, waiters, taxi drivers, room attendants and boat crews. The general rule for waiters, room attendants and boat crews is to tip US$1 per person per day, while porters are tipped US$1 per piece of luggage.

Service charges: Check on arrival at your hotel or resort how they operate regarding service charges. Some automatically add 10% to the final bill, others add 10% if you pay by credit card while some only add 10% to the bar bill.

Accommodation

Most visitors to Maldives are tourists who arrive on a prebooked package to one of the resort islands, arranged by a travel agency in their country of origin. Resorts vary in rating from luxury to mid-range and budget and tourists make their choice prior to departure. On Malé, **hotels** offer comfortable, air-conditioned rooms and en-suite bathrooms with hot and cold fresh running water. **Guesthouses** have sprung up since the early days of tourism. They are now clearly differentiated between Asian, local or foreign accommodation. The budget rooms, with communal bathrooms and no fresh water, are only for Asians and locals while the more upmarket guesthouses cater for foreign tourists

or businessmen. These do not always have hot water but all en-suite bathrooms have fresh running water and either air conditioning or ceiling fans (see Malé At a Glance p. 37).

Eating Out

There is a large selection of restaurants and small tea-shops in Malé. In all the tea shops a wide range of Hedhikaa ('short eats') are available, usually accompanied by tea. Short eats are either sweet or spicy, and tea served tends to be very sweet. During lunch hours (12:00–14:00) and dinner hours (19:00–21:00) most tea shops also serve curry and rice meals. Restaurants that cater to tourists offer Asian, Indian, Chinese, and Western food; many serve Italian cuisine. On each of the resort islands there is a restaurant and some resorts have more than one. Most of the complexes also have a coffee shop which sells fast food and appetizing snacks.

Food is excellent at the luxury resorts but not very appealing at the budget complexes. Restaurants on Malé are not licensed to sell liquor as Maldives is a devout Muslim country. However, liquor is available on all the resort islands, where bars serve a wide variety of mouthwatering cocktails and alcoholic beverages including a range of international beers.

Transport

Transfers to outlying island resorts are often by boat or

CONVERSION CHART		
FROM	**TO**	**MULTIPLY BY**
Millimetres	Inches	0.0394
Metres	Yards	1.0936
Metres	Feet	3.281
Kilometres	Miles	0.6214
Kilometres square	Square miles	0.386
Hectares	Acres	2.471
Litres	Pints	1.760
Kilograms	Pounds	2.205
Tonnes	Tons	0.984
To convert Celsius to Fahrenheit: x 9 ÷ 5 + 32		

seaplane. Resorts supply their own transport to transfer guests. If you have booked a package tour, your mode of transfer will be pre-arranged and included in the price. You can arrange an aerial flip or a boat excursion from your resort or in Malé.

Air: Outlying islands may be reached by air. Two private companies fly to resort islands from the international airport island, Hulhule.

Trans Maldivian Airways, Malé International Airport, tel: 32-5708, fax: 32-3161.

Maldivian Air Taxi, Malé International Airport, Hulhule, tel: 31-5201/2, fax: 31-5203.

Road: Villages and resort islands do not have any form of mechanized road travel as they are so small. However, in the capital city, Malé, and the southernmost island of Gan there are **bicycles**, **scooters** and **motorbikes** for hire.

Taxis: These are available on Malé although you can walk across the island in about 30 minutes. When hiring a taxi make sure that it has air conditioning otherwise you will boil!

New Taxi Service, tel: 31-5656.

Loyal Taxi Service, tel: 31-4545/32-5656.

Kulee Dhaveli, tel: 32-2122.

Comfort Taxi, tel: 32-1313.

Express Taxi, tel: 32-3132.

Road rules and signs: In Maldives, you drive on the left and the general speed limit is 25kph (15mph). Bicycles, motorbikes and scooters travel wherever the

---

PUBLIC HOLIDAYS

1 January • New Year's Day
26 July • Independence Day
3 November • Victory Day
11 November •
Republic Day
December 10 •
Fisherman's Day
17 December • National Day
The other holidays are based on the Islamic lunar calendar and the dates vary every year. These are:
Huravee Day • to celebrate independence from the Portuguese.
Martyr's Day • Maulid (the birthday of the Prophet Muhammed).
Ramadan • the Islamic month of fasting; depends on the sighting of the new moon in Mecca
Kuda Id • end of Ramadan when the new moon rises.

---

driver finds a gap on the road. Traffic lights are now found at the major road junctions. When you arrive at an intersection you slow down but don't necessarily have to stop.

Maps: Road maps of Malé are found in travel guide books which can be bought at any book store or curio shop. Tourist maps of Maldives are also sold in all curio shops.

Buses and trains: There are no buses or trains in Maldives.

Boats: Taxi *dhonis* regularly cross between Hulhule International Airport and Malé. Speedboats and *dhonis* can be hired for journeys to outlying islands.

The resort transfers leave from the airport. Inquire at the port

on Marine Drive on the northern end of Malé Island or call the particular island which you are interested in, for the departure times.

Speedboats may also be chartered for game fishing, transfers or excursions to resort islands. For more information contact: **International Sea Services Maldives**, tel: 32-1198. Also, a new ferry service operates charter-island services from Malé. Contact **Island Ferry Services**, Education Building, Marine Drive, Malé, tel: 31-8252 for more information.

Yachts: Yachtsmen wishing to sail around the islands must clear customs and then apply for a Cruising Permit at the **Ministry of Atolls Administration**, Faashanaa Building, Marine Drive, Malé, tel: 32-3070.

Business Hours

Normal trading and business hours of shops: 09:00–12:30, 13:30–18:00, 20:00–23:00. Teashops: 05:30–01:00. They may close for 15 minutes during prayer.

Time Difference

Throughout the entire year, Maldives Standard Time is five hours ahead of Greenwich Mean (Universal Standard) Time, four hours ahead of European Winter Time, 10 hours ahead of the USA's Eastern Standard Winter Time, five hours behind Sydney, Australia, and four hours behind Japan's Standard Time.

Communications

Malé Post Office, opposite Maldives Port Authorities, Boduthakurufaanu magu, Malé, tel: 32-1558, fax: 32-1559. Facilities include money exchange, courier service (EMS and DHL), money orders and postal transactions. Open 08:15–21:00 Sun–Thu, 09:15–21:00 Sat, 15:00–21:00 Fri and public holidays. Resort islands also sell stamps and post mail for visitors.

Telephones are all satellite linked and all resort islands have telephones. All local fishing villages have telephones. The telephone system is fully automatic, and one can dial direct to most parts of the world. Ask at your hotel reception for dialling codes. Local and long-distance calls are metered. Fax facilities are available at major resorts. **Internet** facilities can be found in Malé, at the airport and at quite a few resorts.

Electricity

220/230 volts AC. 15-amp 3-pin British plugs or 2-pin European plugs are used on the islands. Some hotel rooms have 110 volt outlets. Not all electric shavers will fit hotel and plug points; visitors should seek advice about adapters from a local electrical supplier.

Weights and Measures

The Metric system is used.

Health Precautions

Visitors are responsible for their own arrangements, and are urged to take out medical insurance before departure. Only a few resort islands have a resident doctor, a few have a nurse or a person trained in First Aid. There is a small, private medical centre specializing in diving emergencies on Bandos Island – it has a hyperbaric chamber for diving accidents. Bottled mineral water is available everywhere. Don't drink tap water!

Personal Safety

Due to the strict Islamic law theft is minimal, especially on resort islands, although this does not mean that you should leave your precious belongings lying around in your room. All hotels offer a safety deposit box service and you are advised to use it. The streets are safe.

Emergencies

Ambulance, tel: 102.
Coastal Radio Operator, tel: 182.
Fire Brigade, tel: 118.
Police, tel: 119.
Indira Gandhi Memorial Hospital, tel: 31-6647.
AMDC Clinic (Swiss), tel: 32-5979, fax: 33-3989.
ADK Medical Hospital (Hotline), tel: 31-3553, 32-0436 and 31-0441, fax: 31-335.
Diving and Medical Emergency, Hyperbaric Treatment Centre, Bandos Island Resort, tel: 44-0088, fax: 44-0060.

Etiquette

Maldives is a strict Islamic country and the Muslims are very devout. Topless sunbathing, nudity or immodest dress are disrespectful and offensive to Maldivians and tourists are requested to observe Maldivian customs and traditions.

Language

Maldives has one official language, Dhivehi, which has its own unique form of script. Today, with the increase of tourism and foreign trade, English is gaining importance as a second language, and it is taught at schools, together with Arabic.

Photography

Bring along all the photographic equipment you may require, including batteries. International film brands are expensive and stock may be old. Only Bandos and Paradise Island offer developing and printing facilities and Kuredu Island offers E6 processing.

FURTHER READING

- Anderson, C and Hafiz, A (1987) *Common Reef Fish of Maldives. Parts 1, 2 and 3* (Novelty Printers and Publishers, Maldives).
- Anderson, RC (1992) *A Diver's Guide to the Sharks of the Maldives* (Novelty Press, Malé).
- Debelius, H (2001) *Indian Ocean Reef Guide* (Ikan, Frankfurt).
- Harwood S & Bryning R (2004), *Dive Guide Maldives* (New Holland).
- Lieske, E and Myers, R (1994) *Collins' Pocket Guide to Coral Reef Fishes, Indo-Pacific and Caribbean* (Harper Collins).

INDEX